# THE

# ANTI-SLAVERY CRUSADE

# IN AMERICA

# THE BROTHERHOOD OF THIEVES

*Stephen S. Foster*

Arno Press
&
The New York Times
New York   1969

Reprint edition 1969 by Arno Press, Inc.

\*

Library of Congress Catalog Card No. 79–82190

\*

Reprinted from a copy in the
Columbia University Libraries

\*

Manufactured in the United States of America

THE BROTHERHOOD OF THIEVES

THE

# BROTHERHOOD OF THIEVES;

OR,

## A TRUE PICTURE

OF THE

### AMERICAN CHURCH AND CLERGY:

## A LETTER

TO

### NATHANIEL BARNEY,

OF NANTUCKET.

By STEPHEN S. FOSTER.

CONCORD, N. H.:

PARKER PILLSBURY.

SINGLE COPIES, 25 CENTS; FIVE COPIES, ONE DOLLAR.

1886.

# INTRODUCTORY, BY THE PUBLISHER.

This edition is as near as possible a *fac-simile* of twenty stereotype editions, published and distributed forty years ago in the heat of the moral and peaceful Anti-Slavery conflict, and before the final appeal to bloodshed and slaughter by the slaveholders themselves. How well our thirty years of peaceful agitation and discussion had enlightened the mind and fired the heart of the Northern people against the iniquities and abominations of the slave system was mightily shown in the fact that an army of more than 2,700,000 men gathered and hurled itself as thunderbolts at the Rebellion, crushing it and its blood-besmeared idol, Slavery, down to irrecoverable destruction!

The title-page, to some readers, may seem startling, almost stunning;—but read the subsequent pages, or one half of them, and see whether the book is misnamed; and see, too, with what face anybody can now say that "The church and clergy of that period abolished slavery!" Yet many at this day do say it. Some even go so far as to declare that they could sooner have done it, had not Garrison, Wendell Phillips, and their fanatical and infidel discipleship been in their way.

This little work, and the "*The American Churches the Bulwarks of American Slavery,*" by Hon. James G. Birney, and "*The Church As It Is, the Forlorn Hope of Slavery,*" by Parker Pillsbury, are now reproduced by the author of the last named, and are for sale by him at Concord, N. H.

For prices, see second page of the cover.

P. P.

Concord, N. H., 1886.

# LETTER.

Esteemed Friend:

In the early part of last autumn, I received a letter from you, requesting me to prepare an article for the press in vindication of the strong language of denunciation of the American church and clergy, which I employed at the late Anti-Slavery Convention on your island, and which was the occasion of the disgraceful mob, which disturbed and broke up that meeting. In my answer, I gave you assurance of prompt compliance with your request; but, for reasons satisfactory to myself, I have failed to fulfil my promise up to the present time. The novelty of the occasion has now passed away; the deep and malignant passions which were stirred in the bosoms of no inconsiderable portion of your people, have, doubtless, subsided; but the important *facts* connected with it are yet fresh in the memories of all; and, as the occasion was one of general, not local, interest, and the spirit which was there exhibited was a fair specimen of the general temper and feeling of our country towards the advocates of equal rights and impartial justice, I trust it will not be deemed amiss in me to make it a subject of public notice, even at this late period.

But in the remarks which I propose to make, it will be no part of my object to vindicate myself in the opinion of the public, against the foul aspersions of those whose guilty quiet my preaching may have disturbed. Indeed, to tell the truth, I place a very low estimate on the good opinions of my countrymen—quite as low, I think, as they do on mine, if I may judge from their very great anxiety to have me speak well of them, which I *positively* never can, so long as their national capital is a human flesh-mart, and their chief magistrate is a slave-breeder. The most that I can do is to pledge myself never to mob them, nay, that I will not even be *displeased* with them, for speaking ill of me, while their character remains what it now is. My opponents, among whom rank most of the church and clergy of the country, have disturbed a majority of the meetings which I have attended, within the last nine months, by drunken, murderous mobs, and in several instances, they have inflicted severe injury upon my person; but I value this violence and outrage as proof of their deep conviction of the truth and power of what I say. I deem the *reproach* of such men sufficient praise. And I here tender them my thanks for the high compliment they have so often paid to my opinions, in the extreme measures to which they have resorted to *compel* me to speak in their praise. But so long as their character remains such that I can bestow no commendations, I shall ask none in return.

Nor is it my intention in this letter, to weaken, by explanations, the force of my testimony against the popular religion of our country, for the purpose of allaying the bloody spirit of persecution which has of late characterized the opposition to my course. True, my life is in danger, especially whenever I attempt to utter my sentiments in houses dedicated to what is called the worship of God; but He who has opened to my view other worlds, in which to reap the rewards and honors of a life of toil and suffering in the cause of truth and human freedom in this, has taught me to "be not afraid of them that kill the body, and after that have no more that they can do." Hence I have no pacificatory explanations to offer, no coward disclaimers to make. But I shall aim to present to the comprehension of the humblest individual, into whose hands this letter may chance to fall, a clear and comprehensive view of the intrinsic moral character of that class of our countrymen who claim our respect and veneration, as ministers and followers of the Prince of Peace. I am charged with having done them great injustice in my public lectures, on that and various other occasions. Many of those, who make this charge, doubtless, honestly think so. To correct their error—to reflect on their minds the light which God has kindly shed on mine—to break the spell in which they are now held by the sorcery of a designing priesthood, and prove that priesthood to be a " Brotherhood of Thieves " and the " Bulwark of American Slavery "—is all that I shall aim to do.

But I ought, perhaps, in justice to those who know nothing of my religious sentiments, except from the misrepresentations of my enemies, to say, that I have no feelings of personal hostility towards any portion of the church or clergy of our country. As children of the same Father, they are endeared to me by the holiest of all ties; and I am as ready to suffer, if need be, in defence of their rights, as in defence of the rights of the Southern slave. My objections to them are purely conscientious. I am a firm believer in the Christian religion, and in Jesus, as a divine being, who is to be our final Judge. I was born and nurtured in the bosom of the church, and for twelve years was among its most active members. At the age of twenty-two, I left the allurements of an active business life, on which I had just entered with fair prospects, and, for seven successive years, cloistered myself within the walls of our literary institutions, in "a course of study preparatory to the ministry." The only object I had in view in changing my pursuits, at this advanced period of life, was to render myself more useful to the world, by extending the principles of Christianity, as taught and lived out by their great Author. In renouncing the priesthood and an organized church, and laboring for their overthrow, my object is still the same. I entered them on the supposition that they were, what from a child I had been taught to regard them, the enclosures of Christ's ministers and flock, and his chosen instrumentalities for extending his kingdom on the earth. I have left them from an unresistible conviction, in spite of my early prejudices, that they are a "hold of every foul spirit," and the devices of men to gain influence and power. And, in rebuking their adherents as I do, my only object is to awaken them, if possible, to a sense of their guilt and moral degradation, and bring them to repentance, and a knowledge of the true God, of whom most of them are now lamentably ignorant, as their lives clearly prove.

The remarks which I made at your Convention were of a most grave and startling character. They strike at the very foundation of all our popular ecclesiastical institutions, and exhibit them to the world as the apologists and supporters of the most atrocious system of oppression and wrong, beneath which humanity has ever groaned. They reflect on the church the deepest possible odium, by disclosing to public view the chains and handcuffs, the whips and branding-irons, the rifles and bloodhounds, with which her ministers and deacons bind the limbs and lacerate the flesh of innocent men and defenceless women. They cast upon the clergy the same dark shade which Jesus threw over the ministers of his day, when he tore away the veil beneath which they had successfully concealed their diabolical schemes of personal aggrandizement and power, and denounced them before all the people, as a "den of thieves," as "fools and blind," "whited sepulchres," "blind guides, which strain at a gnat, and swallow a camel," "hypocrites, who devour widows' houses, and for a pretence make long prayers," "liars," "adulterers," "serpents," "a generation of vipers," who could not "escape the damnation of hell." But, appalling and ominous as they were, I am not aware that I gave the parties accused, or their mobocratic friends, any just cause of complaint. They were all spoken in public, in a free meeting, where all who dissented from me were not only invited, but warmly urged, to reply. I was an entire stranger among you, with nothing but the naked truth and a few sympathizing friends to sustain me, while the whole weight of popular sentiment was in their favor. Was the controversy unequal on their part? Were they afraid to meet me with the same honorable weapons which I had chosen? Conscious innocence seldom consents to tarnish its character by a dishonorable defence. Had my charges been unfounded, a refutation of them, under the circumstances, would have been most easy and triumphant. My opponents, had they been innocent, could have acquitted themselves honorably, and overwhelmed their accuser in deep disgrace, without the necessity of resorting to those arguments which appeal only to one's fears of personal harm, and which are certain to react upon their authors, when the threatening danger subsides.

But if all that I have alleged against them be true, is was obviously my right, nay, my imperative duty, to make the disclosures which I did, even though it might be, as you well know it was, at the peril of my life, and the lives of my associates.

In exposing the deep and fathomless abominations of those *pious* thieves, who gain their livelihood by preaching sermons and stealing babies, I am not at liberty to yield to any intimidations, however imposing the source from whence they come. The right of speech—the liberty to utter our own convictions *freely*, at all times and in all places, at discretion, unawed by fear, unembarrassed by force—is the gift of God to every member of the family of man, and should be preserved inviolate; and for one, I can consent to surrender it to no power on earth, but with the loss of life itself. Let not the petty tyrants of our land, in church or state, think to escape the censures which their crimes deserve, by hedging themselves about with the frightful penalties of human law, or the more frightful violence of a drunken and murderous mob. There live the men who are not afraid to die, even though called to meet their fate within the gloomy walls of a dismal prison, with no kind hand to wipe the cold death-sweat from their sinking brow; and they scorn a fetter on *limb* or *spirit*. They know their rights, and know how to defend them, or to obtain more than an equivalent for their loss, in the rewards of a martyr to the right. While life remains, they will speak, and speak *freely*, though it be in "A Voice from the Jail;" nor will they treat the crimes and vices of slave-breeding priests, and their consecrated abettors of the North, with less severity than they do the crimes and vices of other marauders on their neighbors' property and rights. Nor should the friends of freedom be alarmed at the consequences of this faithful dealing with "spiritual wickedness in high places." The mobs which it creates are but the violent contortions of the patient, as the deep gashes of the operator's knife sever the infected limb from his sickly and emaciated body.

The fact that my charges against the religious sects of our country were met with violence and outrage, instead of sound arguments and invalidating testimony, is strong presumptive evidence of their truth. The innocent never find occasion to resort to this disgraceful mode of defence. If our clergy and church were the ministers and church of Christ, would their reputation be defended by drunken and murderous mobs? Are brickbats and rotten eggs the weapons of truth and Christianity? Did Jesus say to his disciples, "Blessed are ye when the *mob* shall speak well of you, and shall defend you?" The church, slavery, and the mob, are a queer trinity! And yet that they are a trinity—that they all "agree in one"—cannot be denied. Every assault which we have made on the bloody slave system, as I shall hereafter show, has been promptly met and repelled by the church, which is herself the claimant of several hundred thousand slaves; and whenever we have attempted to expose the guilt and hypocrisy of the church, the *mob* has uniformly been first and foremost in her defense. But I rest not on presumptive evidence, however strong and conclusive, to sustain my allegations against the American church and clergy. The proof of their identity with slavery, and of their consequent deep and unparalleled criminality, is positive and overwhelming, and is fully adequate to sustain the gravest charges, and to justify the most denunciatory language that has ever fallen from the lips of their most inveterate opponents.

I said at your meeting, among other things, that the American church and clergy, as a body, were thieves, adulterers, manstealers, pirates, and murderers; that the Methodist Episcopal church was more corrupt and profligate than any house of ill-fame in the city of New York; that the Southern ministers of that body were desirous of perpetuating slavery for the purpose of supplying themselves with concubines from among its hapless victims; and that many of our clergymen were guilty of enormities that would disgrace an Algerine pirate!! These sentiments called forth a burst of holy indignation from the *pious* and *dutiful* advocates of the church and clergy, which overwhelmed the meeting with repeated showers of stones and rotten eggs, and eventually compelled me to leave your island, to prevent the shedding of human blood. But whence this violence and personal abuse, not only of the author of these obnoxious sentiments, but also of your own unoffending wives and daughters,

1*

whose faces and dresses, you will recollect, were covered with the most loathsome filth ? It is reported of the ancient Pharisees and their adherents, that they stoned Stephen to death for preaching doctrines at war with the popular religion of their times, and charging them with murder of the Son of God; but their successors of the modern church, it would seem, have discovered some new principle in theology, by which it is made their duty not only to stone the heretic himself, but all those also who may at any time be found listening to his discourse without a permit from their priest. Truly, the church is becoming "terrible as an army with banners."

This violence and outrage on the part of the church were, no doubt, committed to the glory of God and the honor of religion, although the connection between rotten eggs and holiness of heart is not very obvious. It is, I suppose, one of the mysteries of religion which laymen cannot understand without the aid of the clergy ; and I therefore suggest that the pulpit make it a subject of Sunday discourse. But are not the charges here alleged against the clergy strictly and literally true? I maintain that they are true to the very letter; that the clergy and their adherents are literally, and beyond all controversy, a "brotherhood of thieves ; " and, in support of this opinion, I submit the following considerations :—

You will agree with me, I think, that slaveholding involves the commission of all the crimes specified in my first charge, viz., theft, adultery, man-stealing, piracy, and murder. But should you have any doubts on this subject, they will be easily removed by analyzing this atrocious outrage on the laws of God, and the rights and happiness of man, and examining separately the elements of which it is composed. Wesley, the celebrated founder of the Methodists, once denounced it as the " sum of all villanies." Whether it be the sum of *all* villanies, or not, I will not here express an opinion ; but that it is the sum of at least *five*, and those by no means the least atrocious in the catalogue of human aberrations, will require but a small tax on your patience to prove.

1. Theft. To steal, is to take that which belongs to another, without his consent. Theft and robbery are, *morally*, the same act, different only in form. Both are included under the command, " Thou shalt not steal;" that is, thou shalt not take thy neighbor's property. Whoever, therefore, either secretly or by force, possesses himself of the property of another, is a thief. Now, no proposition is plainer than that every man owns his own industry. He who tills the soil has a right to its products, and cannot be deprived of them but by an act of felony. This prin-

ciple furnishes the only solid basis for the right of private or individual property; and he who denies it, either in theory or practice, denies that right, also. But every slaveholder takes the entire industry of his slaves, from infancy to gray hairs; they dig
the soil, but he receives its products. No matter how kind or
humane the master may be,—he lives by plunder. He is emphatically a freebooter; and, as such, he is as much more despicable a character than the common horse-thief, as his depredations
are more extensive,

2. Adultery. This crime is disregard for the requisitions of
marriage. The conjugal relation has its foundation deeply laid
in man's nature, and its strict observance is essential to his happiness. Hence Jesus Christ has thrown around it the sacred
sanction of his written law, and expressly declared that the man
who violates it, even by a lustful eye, is an adulterer. But does
the slaveholder respect this sacred relation? Is he cautious
never to tread upon forbidden ground? No! His very position makes him the minister of unbridled lust. By converting
woman into a commodity to be bought and sold, and used by her
claimant as his avarice or lust may dictate, he totally annihilates
the marriage institution, and transforms the wife into what he
very significantly terms a "BREEDER," and her children into
"STOCK."

This change in woman's condition, from a free moral agent to
a chattel, places her domestic relations entirely beyond her own
control, and makes her a mere instrument for the gratification
of another's desires. The master claims her body as his property, and, of course, employs it for such purposes as best suit his
inclinations,—demanding free access to her bed; nor can she resist his demands but at the peril of her life. Thus is her chastity left entirely unprotected, and she is made the lawful prey of
every pale-faced libertine who may choose to prostitute her!
To place woman in this situation, or to retain her in it when
placed there by another, is the highest insult that any one could
possibly offer to the dignity and purity of her nature; and the
wretch who is guilty of it deserves an epithet compared with
which adultery is spotless innocence. *Rape* is his crime! death
his desert,—if death be ever due to criminals! Am I too severe? Let the offence be done to a sister or daughter of yours;
nay, let the Rev. Dr. Witherspoon, or some other *ordained* miscreant from the South, lay his vile hands on your own bosom companion, and do to her what he has done to the companion of another,—and what Prof. Stuart and Dr. Fisk say he may do,
"without violating the Christian faith,"—and I fear not your reply. None but a moral monster ever consented to the enslave-

ment of his own daughter, and none but fiends incarnate ever enslave the daughter of another. Indeed, I think the demons in hell would be ashamed to do to their fellow-demons what many of our clergy do to their own church members.

3. Man-stealing. What is it to steal a man? Is it not to claim him as your property?—to call him yours? God has given to every man an inalienable right to himself,—a right of which nö conceivable circumstance of birth, or forms of law, can divest him; and he who interferes with the free and unrestricted exercise of that right, who, not content with the proprietorship of his own body, claims the body of his neighbor, is a man-stealer. This truth is self-evident. Every man, idiots and the insane only excepted, knows that he has no possible right to another's body; and he who persists, for a moment, in claiming it, incurs the guilt of man-stealing. The plea of the slave-claimant, that he has bought, or inherited, his slaves, is of no avail. What right had he, I ask, to purchase, or to inherit, his neighbors? The purchase, or inheritance of them as a legacy, was itself a crime of no less enormity than the original act of kidnapping. But every slave-holder, whatever his profession or standing in society may be, lays his felonious hands on the body and soul of his equal brother, robs him of himself, converts him into an article of merchandise, and leaves him a mere chattel personal in the hands of his claimants. Hence he is a kidnapper, or man-thief.

4. Piracy. The American people, by an act of solemn legislation, have declared the enslaving of human beings on the coast of Africa to be piracy, and have affixed to this crime the penalty of death. And can the same act be piracy in Africa, and not be piracy in America? Does crime change its character by changing longitude? Is killing, with malice aforethought, no murder, where there is no human enactment against it? Or can it be less piratical and Heaven-daring to enslave our own native countrymen, than to enslave the heathen sons of a foreign and barbarous realm? If there be any difference in the two crimes, the odds is in favor of the foreign enslaver. Slaveholding loses none of its enormity by a voyage across the Atlantic, nor by baptism into the Christian name. It is piracy in Africa; it is piracy in America; it is piracy the wide world over; and the American slaveholder, though he possess all the sanctity of the ancient Pharisees, and make prayers as numerous and long, is a *pirate* still; a base, profligate adulterer, and wicked contemner of the holy institution of marriage; identical in moral character with the African slave-trader, and guilty of a crime which, if committed on a foreign coast, he must expiate on the gallows.

5. Murder. Murder is an act of the mind, and not of the hand. "Whosoever hateth his brother is a murderer." A man may kill,—that is his hand may inflict a mortal blow,—without committing murder. On the other hand, he may commit murder without actually taking life. The intention constitutes the crime. He who, with a pistol at my breast, demands my pocket-book or my life, is a murderer, whichever I may choose to part with. And is not he a murderer, who, with the same deadly weapon, demands the surrender of what to me is of infinitely more value than my pocket-book, nay, than life itself—my liberty—myself— my wife and children—all that I possess on earth, or can hope for in heaven? But this is the crime of which every slaveholder is guilty. He maintains his ascendency over his victims, extorting their unrequited labor, and sundering the dearest ties of kindred, only by the threat of extermination. With the slave, as every intelligent person knows, there is no alternative. It is submission or death, or, more frequently, protracted torture more horrible than death. Indeed, the South never sleeps, but on dirks, and pistols, and bowie knives, with a troop of bloodhounds standing sentry at every door! What, I ask, means this splendid enginery of death, which gilds the palace of the tyrant master? It tells the story of his guilt. The burnished steel which waits beneath his slumbering pillow, to drink the life-blood of outraged innocence, brands him as a murderer. It proves, beyond dispute, that the submission of his victims is the only reason why he has not already shed their blood.

By this brief analysis of slavery, we stamp upon the forehead of the slaveholder, with a brand deeper than that which marks the victim of his wrongs, the infamy of theft, adultery, man-stealing, piracy, and murder. We demonstrate, beyond the possibility of doubt, that he who enslaves another—that is, robs him of his right to himself, to his own hands, and head, and feet, and transforms him from a free moral agent into a mere *brute*, to obey, not the commands of God, but his claimant—is guilty of every one of these atrocious crimes. And in doing this, we have only demonstrated what, to every reflecting mind, is self-evident. Every man, if he would but make the case of the slave his own, would feel in his inmost soul the truth and justice of this charge. But these are the crimes which I have alleged against the American church and clergy. Hence, to sustain my charge against them, it only remains for me to show that they are slaveholders. That they are slaveholders—party to a conspiracy against the liberty of more than two millions of our countrymen, and as such, are guilty of the crimes of which they stand accused—I affirm, and will now proceed to prove.

It may be necessary for me first, however, to show what constitutes slaveholding, as there seems to be no little confusion in the minds of many on this point. And here let me say, the word itself, if analyzed, will give an accurate description of the act. It is to *hold* one in slavery—to keep him in the condition of a chattel. But slaveholding, in all cases, is necessarily a social crime. A man may commit theft or murder alone, but no *single* individual can ever *enslave* another. It is only when several persons associate together, and combine their influence against the liberty of an individual, that he can be deprived of his freedom, and reduced to slavery. Hence connection with an association, any part of whose object is to hold men in slavery, constitutes one a slaveholder. Nor is the nature or criminality of his offence altered or affected by the number of persons connected with him in such an association. If a million of people conspired together to enslave a solitary individual, each of them is a slaveholder, and no less guilty than if he were alone in the crime. It is no palliation of his offence to say, that he is opposed to slavery. The better feelings of every slaveholder are opposed to slavery. But if he be opposed to it, why, I ask, is he concerned in it? Why does he countenance, aid, or abet, the infernal system? The fact of his opposition to it, in feeling, instead of mitigating his guilt, only enhances it, since it proves, conclusively, that he is not unconscious of the wrong he is doing.

It is a common but mistaken opinion, that, to constitute one a slaveholder, he must be the claimant of slaves. That title belongs alike to the slave-claimant, and all those who, by their countenance or otherwise, lend their influence to support the slave system. If I aid or countenance another in stealing, I am a thief, though he receive all the booty. The Knapps, it will be recollected, were hung as the murderers of Mr. White, though Crowninshield gave the fatal blow, and that, too, while they were at a distance from the bloody scene. It matters little who does the mastery, and puts on the drag-chain and hand-cuffs, whether it be James B. Gray, the Boston Police, Judge Story, or some distinguished Doctor of Divinity of the South; the guilt of the transaction consists in authorizing or allowing it to be done. Hence all who, through their political or ecclesiastical connections, aid or countenance the master in his work of death, are slaveholders, and, as such, are stained with all the moral turpitude which attaches to the man who, by their sanction, wields the bloody lash over the heads of his trembling victims, and buries it deep in their quivering flesh. Nay, the human *hounds* which guard the plantation, ever eager to bark on the track of the flying fugitive, are objects of deeper indignation and abhorrence than even its lordly proprietor.

How stands this matter, then, in regard to the American church and clergy? Is it true of them that they are either claimants of slaves or *watch-dogs* of the plantation? Such, I regret to say, is the shameful and humilitating fact. It is undeniably true, that, with comparatively few exceptions, they occupy one of these two positions in relation to the "peculiar institution." Thousands of the ministers, and tens of thousands of the members of the different sects, are actually claimants of slaves. They buy and sell, mortgage and lease, their own "brethren in the Lord," not unfrequently breaking up families, and scattering their bleeding fragments over all the land, never to be gathered again till the archangel's trump shall wake their slumbering ashes into life. In confirmation of this statement, if proof be asked, I submit the following testimony of Rev. Samuel Heuston, late of Utica, N. Y., an accredited minister of the Methodist Episcopal church, who formerly resided at the South. In reply to several questions by Rev. George Storrs, of the same church, Mr. H. says,—

"I know that members of the M. E. church sell slaves at auction, to the highest bidder; and it is not considered a disciplinary offence. I know of Methodist preachers buying slaves with no apparent design to better their condition, but evidently for the sake of gain.

"I should think nearly one half, at least, of the ministers of our church hold slaves and trade in them; and nearly all the members, who are able to own slaves, not only hold them, but buy and sell them.

"I know an official member of the M. E. church, Col. ———, that bought in one purchase about *fifty thousand dollars'* worth of slaves.

"Esq. ———, of ———, S. C., an official member of the M. E. church, who made it a business to buy and sell slaves in lots to suit the purchasers, has became rich by his speculation in them, and still continues his trade in human beings—trading not only for himself, but as an agent for others. *His house is head-quarters for Methodists—a home for the preachers. He is a chief man in the church; very benevolent.*"

The opinion of Mr. Heuston as to the extent to which the Methodists are engaged in breeding and trafficking in slaves, is corroborated by the testimony of Rev. James Smylie, a Presbyterian clergyman of Mississippi, who affirms the same thing of all the other large denominations. In a pamphlet which he published in defence of slavery, in 1838, I think it was, we find the following passage :—

" If slavery be a sin, and advertising and apprehending slaves with a view to restore them to their masters, is a direct violation of the divine law, and if *the buying, selling, or holding a slave,* FOR THE SAKE OF GAIN, is a heinous sin and scandal, then, verily, THREE FOURTHS OF ALL THE EPISCOPALIANS, METHODISTS, BAPTISTS, and PRESBYTERIANS, in ELEVEN STATES OF THE UNION, are of the devil. They ' hold,' if they do not buy and sell slaves, and, *with few exceptions,* they hesitate not to ' apprehend and restore ' runaway slaves when in their power.''

The statements of these individuals apply to the South only. It is only in that portion of the country that Mr. S. says, and says truly, that if slavery be a sin (and no man doubts that it is), three fourths of all the Episcopalians, Methodists, Baptists, and Presbyterians are of the devil. But as the Northern branch of the church is much larger than the Southern, a large majority of the ministers and church members of the whole country hold no property in slaves. But while it is true they are not claimants of slaves, it is equally true that they are the apologists and supporters of the system. For the sake of union with the South, the Northern church and clergy, in concert with non-professors, have made their respective states hunting-grounds for Southern kidnappers, and themselves the hounds. They have covenanted with the South that whenever one of her slaves shall make his escape to Massachusetts, Judge Story and the United States marshal, with his *posse comitatus,* shall dog him down, secure his person, and in due time deliver him up to the original kidnapper. Nor is this all. They have consented to become the body-guard of the slave-master, and have pledged themselves to protect him against every attempt of his slaves to throw off their chains.

It is to this union and pledge of protection from the North, that the slave system owes its perpetuity to the present time. Such, at least, is the opinion of the slave-claimants themselves. Hence they shriek out in dismay at the first proposition of the abolitionists to dissolve the Union, and leave them alone in the enjoyment of their peculiar institutions. Such, too, is the opinion of every man of sense who knows anything of the past history or present condition of our slave population. The North, as he very well knows, are emphatically the slave-*holders.* They are the soldiers who *level the musket,* as the South gives the word of command. Indeed, to satisfy himself of this, the humblest and most uninformed of our citizens needs but little reflection on the facts already within his knowledge. Who does not know that in this country are two and a half millions of people who are doomed to a state of " bondage, one hour of which is fraught with more misery than ages of that which our fathers rose in rebellion to oppose "? Confederated with them are not less than half a million of abolitionists, and free people of color, who believe in the right and duty of self-defence, and who are ready to join in every feasible measure to secure their liberty. Now I ask by whose agency this vast people are kept in their present horrible condition. To say that they are held by their claimants, would be to talk like one bereft of his reason. They are but a mere handful of men, at most, less than three hundred thousand, or, on an average, about one to every ten slaves. From this vast inequality in numbers it is certain that their masters are not alone concerned in their enslavement. To keep a million of robust, athletic men and women in a state of abject servitude, requires a force far beyond what they are competent to furnish. Whence, then, comes that force? Who are the allies and abettors of these horrible tyrants, who live upon the blighted hopes of prostrate millions? Are they the crowned despots of the old world? Have Algiers and Constantinople disgorged themselves, and sent forth swarms of troops to form a living, impregnable bulwark around these execrable monsters, and shield them from the righteous indignation of outraged humanity? The South herself shall answer this question. She shall speak, and disclose her accomplices in this work of death.

Says the editor of the Maryville (Tenn.) *Intelligencer*, in an article on the character and condition of the slave population,—

" We of the South are emphatically surrounded by a dangerous class of beings,—degraded, stupid savages,—who, if they could but once entertain the idea that immediate and unconditional death would not be their portion, would react the St. Domingo tragedy. But the consciousness, with all their stupidity, that a tenfold force, superior in discipline if not in barbarity, would gather from the four corners of the United States, and slaughter them, keeps them in subjection. *But to the non-slaveholding states, particularly, we are indebted for a permanent safeguard against insurrection.* Without their assistance, the white population of the South would be too weak to quiet that innate desire for liberty which is ever ready to act itself out with every rational creature."

In a debate in Congress on the resolution to censure John Quincy Adams for presenting a petition for the dissolution of the Union, Mr. Underwood of Kentucky made the following very just confession—a confession which concedes all that I have ever claimed in regard to the guilt of the North, and which the church and the clergy must disprove, or admit all that I have alleged against them. In speaking of the effect of a repeal of the Union on slavery, Mr. U. said,—

"They (the South) were the weaker portion, were in the minority. The North could do what they pleased with them ; they could adopt their own measures. All he asked was, that they would let the South know what those measures were. One thing he knew well—that the state which he in part represented, had perhaps a deeper interest in this subject than any other, except Maryland and a small portion of Virginia. And why? Because he knew that to dissolve the Union, and separate the different states composing this confederacy,—making the Ohio river, and Mason and Dixon's line, the boundary line,—he knew as soon as that was done, *slavery was done*, in Kentucky, Maryland, and a large portion of Virginia, and it would extend to all the states south of this line. *The dissolution of the Union was the dissolution of slavery.* It had been the common practice for Southern men to get up on this floor, and say, 'Touch this subject, and we will dissolve this Union as a remedy.' Their remedy was the destruction of the thing which they wished to save, and any sensible man could see it. If the Union were dissolved into two parts, the slave would cross the line, and then turn round and curse his master from the other shore."

This confession of Mr. Underwood, as to the entire dependence of the slave masters on the citizens of the nominally free states to guard their plantations and secure them against desertion, is substantially confirmed by Thomas D. Arnold, of Tennessee, who, in a speech on the same subject, assures us that they are equally dependent on the North for *personal protection* against their slaves. In assigning his reasons for adhering to the Union, Mr. Arnold makes use of the following remarkable language :

"The free states had now a majority of 44 in that house. Under the new census they would have 53. The cause of the slave-holding states was getting weaker and weaker, and what were they to do? He would ask his Southern friends what the South had to rely on, if the Union were dissolved ? Suppose the dissolution could be peaceably effected (if that did not involve a contradiction of terms), what had the South to depend upon ? *All the crowned heads were against her. A million of slaves were ready to rise and strike for freedom at the first tap of the drum.* They were cut loose from their friends at the North (friends they ought to be, and without them the South had no friends), *whither were they to look for protection ?* How were they to sustain an assault from England, or France, with that cancer at their vitals ? The more the South reflected, the more clearly she must see that she had a deep and vital interest in maintaining the Union."

Testimony to the same effect might be multiplied to an indefinite extent. But more in unnecessary. Every person, acquainted with the politics of the country, knows that slavery is incorporated into the constitution of our government, and is made a part of its settled policy. I have already said that slaveholding was, necessarily, a social crime; that it was only by means of a social organization, by which the power of a whole community could be combined and concentrated on a given point, at a given time, that the liberty of an individual could be crushed. The federal and state governments, linked together as they now are, constitute such an organization. The protection of the slave system was one of the objects for which the Union was formed. By the terms of the federal compact, the citizens of every state in the Union are required and pledged to protect the slave claimants, in each of the states where slavery exists, against any attempt of their slaves to regain their liberty by a resort to arms. The army, the navy, and the militia, of the whole country, are placed at the bidding of the slave power; and every officer in them, from the highest to the lowest, is put under oath to fight the battles of slavery at the master's call. Already have the United States troops been twice employed (at South Hampton, Va., and at Wilmington, N. C.), to suppress insurrection among the slaves; and a call is now made upon the country for a large increase of the navy, for the better protection of the " peculiar institution." The Florida war also furnishes another and more recent instance in which the nation, as such, has unsheathed the sword in defence of slavery. The sole object of that war, which has cost the country more than 7000 lives, and exhausted its treasury of $40,000,000, be it remembered, was the recapture of fugitive slaves, and to prevent further escapes. And the same mighty influence which has exterminated the poor Indian in the everglades of Florida for making his rude wigwam a refuge and home for the panting fugitive, is now waiting to " gather in tenfold force from the four corners of the United States, and slaughter " the pining bondmen of the South, should they attempt to throw off their chains, and assert their right to liberty.

The guaranty of personal security against their slaves, given by the North to the slave-claimants, is the very life-blood of the slave system. Divested of the protection of Northern bayonets, the slave power could not sustain itself a single hour, as the South herself is forced to admit. " Suppose the Union to be dissolved, what has the South to depend upon ? All the crowned heads are against her. A million of slaves are ready to rise and strike for freedom at the first tap of the drum." And why, I ask, do they not *now* rise ? Not, surely, because, in a country like ours, such a step would be deemed morally wrong. The doctrine taught in all our pulpits, and received by the church universally, is, that "resistance to tyrants is obedience to God." Our clergy tell us that self-defence, and the protection of our families, is a duty which we may not innocently neglect, while they denounce non-resistance as the "doctrine of devils." Why, then, do not the slaves assert their freedom, and meet the invaders of their rights in mortal combat, as our fathers did ? Why is not Madison Washington, George Washington? And why are not Charles Remond and Frederic Douglas and Lundsford Lane, the Henrys and Hancocks and Adamses of a second American Revolution ?

But one answer can be given to this question, and that is the one already given by the Maryville *Intelligencer.* The consciousness that, in a controversy with their masters, they must meet the combined forces, military and naval, of the whole country, alone deters them from such a movement. It is not the lily-fingered aristocracy of the South that they fear, as the South herself tells us, but the "white slaves" of the North, who have basely sold themselves for scullions to the slave power, and who are always ready to do the bidding of their haughty proprietors, whatever service they may require at their hands. The slaves know too well, that, should they unfurl the banner of freedom, and demand the recognition of their liberty and rights at the point of the bayonet, the *Northern* pulpit, aghast with holy horror at the incendiary measure, would raise the maddening cry of *insurrection*—the *Northern* church, animated by a kindred spirit, and echoing the infamous libel, would pour forth her sons in countless hordes, and a mighty avalanche of *Northern* soldiery, well disciplined for their work of death by long experience in *Northern* mobs, would rush down upon them from our *Northern* hills in exterminating wrath, and sweep away, in its desolating ruins, the last vestige of their present "forlorn hope!" Do I misrepresent the church and clergy? No! You, at least, know that this would be but to redeem their plighted faith. They stand before the world and before high Heaven sworn to protect every slave-breeder in the land in his *lawful* business of rearing men and women for the market ; nor have they, as a body, ever shown any symptoms of intention to violate the requirements of their oath. They preach and practice allegiance to a government which is based upon the bones and sinews, and cemented with the blood, of millions of their countrymen, and hold themselves in readiness to execute its every decree, at the point of the bayonet. Thus emphatically are they the *holders* of the slaves—the bulwarks of the bloody slave system—and as such, at their hands, if there be any truth in Christianity, will God require the blood of every slave in our land. And, for one, so long as they continue in their present position, I deem it the duty of every friend of humanity to brand them as a Brotherhood of thieves, adulterers, man-stealers, pirates, and murderers, and to prove to the world that, in sustaining the slave system, they do actually commit all these atrocious crimes.

The Federal Compact contains another provision, as I have already intimated, which, in its operation, is no less fatal to the liberties of our enslaved countrymen than that which we have just considered; and one which implicates every friend and supporter of the Union in all the guilt and moral turpitude of slaveholding. I refer to that article of the Constitution which requires the surrender of fugitive slaves. If the Northern States were *really* free, the slaves would forthwith escape into them, and slavery would soon become extinct by emigration, as Mr. Underwood has well said. But what is now the fact? Is there liberty for the slave anywhere within the borders of the United States? When he steps upon the soil of Pennsylvania, or New York, or Massachusetts, do his shackles fall? Can he stand erect, and say, "I am free?" No! He is still a crouching slave—still clanks his chains, and starts affrighted at the crack of the driver's whip. Hotly pursued by the human hounds, which, like the fabled vulture of Prometheus, have long gorged themselves upon his vitals, he reaches forth his imploring hands to the professed ministers and followers of the meek and loving Saviour, and, with looks that would draw tears from adamant, beseeches them by all that is endearing in the ties of our common nature, and by all that is horrible in the doom of a recaptured slave, to save him from the fangs of these terrible monsters. But what is their reply? "Go back"—shame, shame on the church!—"Go back, and wear your chains! True, 'all men are created equal, and endowed by their Creator with certain inalienable rights, among which are life, liberty, and the pursuit of happiness;' and God said 'Thou shalt not deliver to his master the servant which is escaped from his master unto thee'—but—but—but we have covenanted with the wretches who have robbed you of these rights, never to give you shelter, nor protection; but to return you, if found within our borders, again into their power!"

This is no picture of the fancy, as thousands of our unhappy countrymen would testify from sad experience, if they could but speak. Indeed, it is the language of every citizen of the North who holds any other relation to the Federal Compact than that which George Washington and the first American Congress held to the colonial edicts of George III; for that instrument, as interpreted by the Supreme Court, pledges all who assent to it to withhold protection from every man who is claimed as a fugitive slave, and allow him to be dragged 'back into bondage. But have the Northern church and clergy ever refused to fulfil the requisitions of this infamous compact with Southern man-stealers? Have they trampled its provisions under their feet, and indignantly demanded its repeal? Never! On the contrary, with comparatively few exceptions, they have ranged themselves in one of the two great political parties which have long vied with each other in their support of slavery, and at the same time have waged an exterminating warfare against every movement in favor of universal freedom. In connection with these parties, they have kidnapped and returned into slavery vast numbers of those who, at different periods, had been so fortunate as to escape from the power of their masters; and in more instances than one have they indicted and imprisoned abolitionists for giving them succor. Thus have the church and clergy of the North voluntarily consented to become the watch-dogs of the plantation; and from long and intimate acquaintance with their fidelity in this service, I have no hesitation in recommending them to their Southern masters as worthy candidates for the honors of a *brass collar*. And if I were to specify cases of extraordinary merit in this regard, I should name Chief Justice Shaw and Judge Story, and the clergy generally of the city of Boston, as especially entitled to remembrance by James B. Gray, for their prompt and cordial acquiescence in his recent claim of George Latimer. It would be but an act of *justice* in Mr. G. to expend a part of the money for which he sold George in collars, inscribed with the initials of his own name, for these distinguished kidnappers. Their conduct on that occasion, as I can testify from personal observation, richly entitles them to some such lasting memento of their loyalty to the slave power.

There is another view of this subject, which presents the guilt of the Northern church and clergy in a still more glaring light. It is this: To legalize crime, and throw around it the sanction of statutory enactments, is, undeniably, an act of much greater wickedness than to perpetrate it after it has been made lawful. Thus the members of a legislative body, which should enact a law authorizing theft or murder, would more deserve the penitentiary, or gallows, than the man who merely steals, or, in a fit of anger, takes his neighbor's life. The former justify crime, and make it honorable, and thus obliterate all distinction between virtue and vice; the latter merely commits it, when legalized, but attempts no justification of his offence. But the religious professions of the country have legalized slavery, and the infernal slave trade, in the District of Columbia, and in the Territory of Florida! They have made their national capital one of the greatest slave marts on the globe; and they now hold in slavery, by direct legislation, more than thirty thousand human beings, whom they have sternly refused to emancipate. No sect can claim exemption from this charge. In whatever else they differ, they have all united, without exception, by the almost unanimous voice of their members, in opposing the abolition of slavery in those places where they have the power to emancipate, and have declared to the world, by their vote (the most effective way in which they could speak on the subject), that it was their sovereign will and pleasure that the traffic in human beings, which they have branded as piracy on the coast of Africa, should be lawful and honorable commerce in the United States; and that the capital of this land of boasted freedom should be the Guinea Coast of America. Not a mother has been robbed of her babe within the District of Columbia, not a solitary woman has been sold there, without the legal sanction of more than seven eighths of every religious sect of the North. Even the Free-Will Baptists and the Quakers, with all their professed abhorrence of slavery, and their numerous public testimonies against it, in consideration of the paltry sum of four hundred dollars paid into their national treasury, license the auctioneer in human flesh in the city of Washington. I charge this offence upon these denominations, because the immediate agents in granting these licenses are men of their own choice, and men, too, who were selected with the full knowledge of the fact that they were in favor of legalizing the slave-trade, and, if elected to office, would license it in the District of Columbia. The abolitionists have long and earnestly besought the pretended ministers and followers of Christ, of the different sects, to elect men to office who would abolish all legal enactments in favor of slavery, wherever they had the power to do it; but their entreaties have been totally disregarded, and themselves treated with the most profound contempt.

The nature and enormities of the domestic slave-trade which is now carried on in the District of Columbia, on an extensive scale, under the legal sanction of nearly the entire body of the church and clergy, may be seen in the following eloquent and just description of it from a Southern pen. The language is severe, but it is the severity of truth. The only fault I find with it is, that its heaviest strokes are not aimed at those who have thrown the shield of government around this infernal traffic, and made it lawful and honorable commerce. I copy it:

*[From the Millennial Trumpeter, Tenn.]*

" Droves of negroes, chained together in dozens and scores, and hand-cuffed, have been driven through our country in numbers far surpassing any previous year. And these vile slave-drivers and dealers are swarming like buzzards round a carrion, throughout this country. You cannot pass a few miles in the great roads without having every feeling of humanity insulted and lacerated by this spectacle. Nor can you go into any county, or any neighborhood, scarcely, without seeing or hearing of some of these despicable creatures, called negro-drivers.

" Who is a negro-driver? One whose eyes dwell with delight on lacerated bodies of helpless men, women, and children ; whose soul feels diabolical raptures at the chains, and handcuffs, and cart-whips, for inflicting tortures on weeping mothers torn from helpless babes, and on husbands and wives torn asunder forever. Who is a negro-driver? An execrable demon, who is only prevented by want of power, fellow-citizens, from driving your wives, and sons, and daughters, in chains and hand-cuffs, with the blood-stained cart-whip to market. Yea, his hardened heart would make but little difference, whether he made his ill-gotten gain by selling them to a merciless cotton or sugar grower, or by sending them directly to the flames of hell. Is your insulted humanity, ye sons of Tennessee, your insulted sense of right and wrong, your abused conviction of the rights of man, satisfied by saying the tears, and groans, and blood of these human droves are not the tears, and groans, and blood of our wives, children, brothers, and fathers ; or these ' blood-snuffing vultures ' of hell should not set their polluted tread on our soil with impunity? Their lives should atone for their audacity. And is the fountain of your sympathies dried up for the poor oppressed African, merely because he is helpless and defenceless ? Is the hand of efficient aid drawn back, merely because the enchained, bleeding victim cannot help himself? Is not the African thy brother ? Is he not a man, with all the sympathies and sensibilities of our nature ? Was he not made in the image of God ? Did not Christ die to redeem him ? And shall we suffer these miscreant fiends to drive our fellow-men in chains before our eyes, as brutes are driven to market ?

" The laws, you say, protect these ruffians in their nefarious traffic. Yea, the laws are often made by wretches whose characters are frequently a *fac simile* of these negro-drivers, whose moral picture would darken the black canvass of the pit. There are, at this very time, miscreants engaged in this trade, who once polluted our legislative halls. But suppose villains enough of the right hue let into the legislature, and pass laws that one order of society may violate the honor of your wives and daughters; would such a law on the pages of our statute-book secure the perpetrator from condign punishment? What can the dead letter of a statute-book do, in opposition to the public opinion of an enlightened and virtuous community?"

Dark and revolting as is the picture which I have here drawn, there yet remains to be added another shade of still deeper hue. Through whose agency was it, I ask, that a *thief* now fills the presidential chair? John Tyler, the present head and representative of the federal government, is a veteran slave-breeder—a negro-thief of the old Virginia school, who has long supported his own family in princely luxury by desolating the domestic hearthstones of his defenceless neighbors, and whose crimes in this regard, had they been perpetrated North instead of South, of Mason's and Dixon's line, would have consigned him to the state's prison for at least two centuries, or until released by death from his ignominious confinement. Of Mr. Tyler's cabinet, a majority are negro thieves—five of the judges of the Supreme Court are negro thieves—the president of the United States Senate is a negro thief—the speaker of the House of Representatives is a negro thief—the officer first in command in the U. S. army is a negro thief—a majority of all our ministers to foreign courts are negro thieves. And yet these men were all elected to office by the votes, direct or indirect, of the great body of the Northern church and clergy. But why have the clergy and their adherents shown this preference for thieves to rule the nation, and shape its destinies? Doubtless, because they are a "brotherhood of thieves," as like always seeks its like. Away, then, with all their pretensions to Christianity, or even *common honesty*. The man who votes with either of the great political parties does necessarily and inevitably legalize slavery, both of these parties being pledged not only to execute all the provisions of the Constitution in favor of slavery, but to go even farther, and perpetuate the system, with all its abominations, in the District of Columbia; the man who legalizes slavery, and throws around it the protecting shield of the government, is the most guilty and atrocious of slaveholders; and every slaveholder, as I have already shown, is guilty of the crimes of theft, adultery, manstealing, piracy, and murder. It follows, then, as a legitimate and certain conclusion, that as the ministers and members of the Northern church, with comparatively few exceptions, have ranged themselves in the ranks of the Whig or Democratic party,

2

and have thus not only voluntarily formed a political alliance with the slave-claimants, in all the different states of the Union, guaranteeing their personal security, and the return of their fugitive slaves, but have also given their direct sanction to slavery, by legalizing it, and refusing to emancipate those whom they have a constitutional right to set free, they are slaveholders in the most odious sense of this term, and, as such, are guilty of all the crimes alleged against them in my first charge.

From the conclusion to which we have here arrived there is no possible escape. Two and a half millions of our countrymen, now loaded with chains and fetters, demand their liberty at our hands. Shall they be free? What say the Northern church and clergy? By voting for men to rule the country who are known to be the uncompromising opponents of abolition, they answer—No! By refusing to annul that portion of the Federai Compact which requires them to return fugitives from slavery, and put down the slaves, should they attempt to regain their liberty by a resort to arms, they answer—No! By stifling the voice of free discussion, and stirring up mobs against the abolitionists, they answer—No! Whatever influence they possess, as citizens, is all thrown into the scale of slavery. They looked upon John Tyler as he robbed the frantic mother of her babe, and forthwith made him president of the United States! They have seen Henry Clay and John C. Calhoun tear the tender and confiding wife from the fond embrace of her husband, and sell her to a stranger, and they are now eager to confer on them the same splendid honors! And at this very moment, they stand, with sword in hand, ready to thrust it into the heart of the slave, should he assert his freedom and extend the hand of protection to his insulted and outraged wife and daughters!

Should these charges chance to meet the eye of the guilty authors of this wrong, they will doubtless ask, "Is thy servant a dog that he should do this great thing?" YES, I answer, emphatically, ye are *dogs*—the *watch-dogs of your Southern masters, whose plantations ye guard*—and as such, ye are more brutal and inhuman than the servant of the Syrian king. Ye daily rob more than three hundred of your own country-women of their new-born babes, and doom those babes to a fate more horrible than *death*, breaking the mother's heart! Ye have recklessly trampled under foot the sacred institution of marriage, consigned every sixth woman in the country to a life of hopeless concubinage and adultery, and turned your famous Ten-Miles Square into a mart where the rich aristocrat may lawfully sell the poor man's wife for purposes of prostitution, thus legalizing violence on female chastity in its most horrible and disgusting forms. Think, ye fathers and mothers, against whom I bring these tremendous charges; O, think of your own daughters on the block of the auctioneer, to be sold to any vile and loathsome wretch who may choose to purchase them, to pander to his beastly lusts! See your own darling son, in the person of George Latimer, kidnapped in open day, in the heart of New England's metropolis, and under the very eye of her pulpit: behold him manacled in open court, and dragged in chains through the streets of that proud city, not by a drunken mob; but by the police, with the city marshal at their head; and finally immured with felons in a dismal cell, there to wait, for weeks, with trembling anxiety, the horrible doom of a recaptured slave—and tell me if they are not *dogs*, nay, *fiends incarnate*, who perpetrate such outrages! But remember, "*Thou* art the man!" What I have here supposed to be done to thy son and daughters, *thou* hast done to the son and daughters of another!

No intelligent person, man or woman, who is in concert with the Whig or Democratic party, or who votes for any other than an uncompromising abolitionist for civil office, or silently countenances such voting, can say, in truth, he is innocent of these crimes. It is impossible! Sooner will Pontius Pilate shake from his spotted robes the blood of the murdered Jesus; sooner, far sooner, will the infatuated Jew, who cried "Away with him, away with him, let him be crucified," stand acquitted before the bar of his final Judge, than such a man exculpate himself from the guilt of slavery. In imitation of the Roman judge, he may wash his hands before the people by passing resolves against slavery, or excluding slave-claimants from his communion table, and say, "I am innocent of the blood of the slave;" but it is of no avail. Still in his " skirts is found the blood of the souls of the poor innocents." For private ends, he continues to sustain, by his vote, a system which, in words, he has repudiated, as the supple tool of the envious Pharisees condemned to death the man whom he had previously pronounced without a fault; and hence, in his ecclesiastical condemnation of slavery, he only adds to the crime of slaveholding the guilt of base hypocrisy. So long as a solitary slave shall leave his foot-prints on our soil, or clank his chains in our ears, no position can be innocent, nor safe, but that of uncompromising hostility to whatever is in fellowship or alliance with the slave power; and they alone who have assumed this position can justly claim exemption from the charge of slaveholding.

I might pursue the political aspect of this subject still farther, and bring together a great amount of additional proof in support of my positions. But it is needless. Indeed more evidence would only lumber and confuse the mind, instead of aiding its conclusions. I will, therefore, conclude with a single additional consideration.

The remark which I wish to add is this: The clerical and lay members, with few exceptions, of all the various religious sects in the country, are identified with one of the two great political parties which administer and control the government, either by actually voting for their candidates, or by a silent acquiescence in, and approval of, their measures. Those clergymen who absent themselves from the polls, but fail to rebuke the members of their respective churches for voting with those parties in support of slavery, are as responsible for their votes as they would be had they deposited them in the ballot-box with their own hands. This, at least, is the doctrine of the ancient prophet: *"When I say unto the wicked, O wicked man, thou shalt surely die; if thou dost not speak to warn the wicked from his way, that wicked man shall die in his iniquity; but his blood will I require at thine hand."* [Ezekiel xxxiii, 8.] Hence, politically, the sects are Whig and Democrat; and up to this hour they have gone all lengths with these parties, in their "Tippecanoe and Tyler, too," and "Kinderhook" conventions for the election of slave-masters, and "Northern men with Southern principles," to fill the highest offices in the gift of the people. Now, I ask, were their own children in slavery, would they be found in the ranks of these parties? If you say, Yea, then I reply, Would they honor with the highest offices in the government the men who had debauched their own daughters, and sold the flesh, and bones, and blood of their sons in human shambles? If you say, Nay; then, without further argument, are they individually convicted of knowingly and intentionally contributing of their influence to support the slave system—a system that robs two and a half millions of our countrymen of every right and privilege which renders life a blessing; and therefore they must answer to God, not for the enslavement of one or two individuals merely, but of every victim of our country's wrongs who now pines in his chains. And if Christianity be not a fable, Christ will say to them in the day of judgment, not only for what they have actually done to sustain slavery, but for what they have neglected to do for its overthrow, "I was a hungered, and ye gave me no meat; I was thirsty, and ye gave me no drink; I was a stranger, and ye took me not in; naked, and ye clothed me not; sick and in prison,"—*down on the plantations of the South*—"and ye visited me not." "Depart from me, ye cursed, into everlasting fire, prepared for the devil and his angels." For, "Verily I say unto you, inasmuch as ye did it not to one of the least of these, ye did it not to me."

In the former part of my letter, I have shown that slavery is an American and not a Southern institution, and that the North and South are leagued together politically in its support. I have also shown, both by reference to facts, and from the testimony of distinguished men at the South, that the slave power could not sustain itself a single hour without the aid and protection of the general government, but must fall at once before the avenging arm of its outraged victims; and, consequently, that all who sustain the government in its present pro-slavery character, do thereby sustain the slave system, and should be held responsible for all the guilt and misery which it involves. But while the federal government, that is, the electors of the country, are the direct and visible agents on whose authority and fostering care slavery depends for support and perpetuity, there is, in this case, as in most others of a like nature, "a power behind the throne greater than the throne itself;" for in a country like ours, civil government is of no force, any farther than it is sustained by popular sentiment. The will of the people for the time being is the supreme law of the land, the legislative and executive departments of the government being nothing more than a mere echo of the popular will. Hence the power which controls public opinion does, in fact, give laws to our country, and is, therefore, preëminently responsible for the vices which are sanctioned by those laws. That power in this case, is the priesthood, backed up and supported by the church. They are the manufacturers of our public sentiment; and, consequently, they hold in their hand the key to the great prison-house of Southern despotism, and can " open and no man shut, and shut and no man open."

There are in our country more than twenty thousand of this class of men, scattered over every part of the land, and at the same time so united in national and local associations as to act in perfect harmony, whenever concert is required. They constitute what may properly be termed a *religious aristocracy.* Among the exclusive privileges which they claim and enjoy, is the right to administer the ordinances of religion, and to lead in all our religious services. The ear of the nation is open to them every seventh day of the week, when they pour into it just such sentiments as they choose. And not only are they in direct and constant contact with the people in their public ministrations, but in their parochial visits, at the sick bed, at weddings, and at funerals, all of which are occasions when the mind is peculiarly tender, and susceptible of deep and lasting impressions. Amply supported by the contributions of the church, their whole time is devoted to the work of moulding and giving character to public sentiment; and with the advantages which they enjoy over all other classes of society, of leisure, the sanctity of their office, and direct and constant contact with the people as their "spiritual guides," their power has become all-controlling. It is in a *finite* sense omnipresent in every section of the country, and is absolutely *irresistible*, wherever their claims are allowed. Hence, what they countenance, it will be next to an impossibility to overthrow, at least till their order itself be overthrown; and whatever system of evil they oppose, must melt away like snow beneath the warm rays of an April sun.

To illustrate the strength of their power more fully, I will suppose a case. The car of temperance rolls back its ponderous wheels, and we become a nation of drunkards. Midnight gloom covers the whole land. The voice of the reformer is no longer heard in stern rebuke against the general debauch which is now rife in every rank and grade of society. The traffic in intoxicating drinks is legalized in all parts of the country, and by a law of Congress for the District of Columbia, every person who visits the seat of government on business, or for pleasure, may be compelled to drink to intoxication, on penalty of thirty-nine lashes on his bare back, inflicted at discretion of the rum-sellers of the district.

In this state of things, suddenly some daring spirit starts up, and with the watchword of reform gathers around him a little band of fearless coadjutors, who, with himself, pledge their lives, their fortunes, and their sacred honor, to the glorious work of delivering the country from the scourge and curse of intemperance. Struck with the sanctity of their professions, they naturally look to the priesthood and church for aid and coöperation. But to their surprise, they find that thousands of the clergy are not only the victims, but the apologists and advocates, of this degrading vice and crime; many of them among the best customers of the rum-seller; they often go reeling and staggering from the grog-shop to the meeting-house, and are obliged to ascend the pulpit on borrowed feet; and it not unfrequently occurs, during the divine services of the Sabbath, that the sentiments of melting tenderness, which flow forth in supplication from the *pious* heart of the officiating priest, are interrupted in their passage by a sudden explosion of the contents of the decanter from his surcharged stomach. Deacons, too, in countless numbers, are drunkards; the communion season is often a Bacchanalian revel; and much of the revenues of the church is the profits of the distillery. Doctors of divinity and presidents of our theological seminaries are often found engaged in amassing wealth by rumselling; and not a few of the members and officers of the American Board of Commissioners for Foreign Missions, and of the American Bible Society, are addicted to habitual intoxication; while the entire body of the priesthood and church, of all denominations, are united in electing to the highest offices in the gift of the people men who are not only notorious drunkards, but who are also known to be in favor of perpetuating the infamous law, in the District of Columbia, which allows the rumsellers of the district to compel the citizens of the place, and strangers from abroad, to drink to intoxication, or submit to thirty-nine lashes on their bare backs.

Schooled in the philosophy of the apostle who taught that "judgment must begin at the house of God," the reformers call first upon the church and priesthood to repent, and sign the pledge of total abstinence. A few comply with the call, and not only sign the pledge, but advocate its merits; but much the larger portion continue to drink; and to save their own reputation, they pour contempt and ridicule on the friends of total abstinence, and wink at the mobs which are got up to put them down. Presbyteries resolve that drunkenness "is not opposed to the will of God." The General Conference of the Methodist Episcopal church declare, by an overwhelming vote, that they have no "right, wish, or intention" to abolish intemperance. Professor Stuart comes out in a published letter, and denounces the lectures on total abstinence as mere "spoutings and vehemence," and boldly declares that men may get drunk "without violating the Christian faith, or the church." President Fisk endorses this doctrine, and asserts that it "will stand, because it is Bible doctrine." Some of the smaller sects, and local bodies in the more influential ones, pass resolutions in favor of temperance; but at the same time slander and traduce its firmest and most unflinching friends, because they refuse to recognize a rum-drinking and rum-selling church and clergy as the representatives and followers of Christ; and, as if to give undoubted proof of their hypocrisy, they still continue to vote for drunkards and the advocates of the compulsion law for the presidency and and all other important offices in the gift of the people, and sternly resist every importunity of the friends of temperance to aid in the election of men who are in favor of repealing that infernal enactment.

Now, with the church and clergy in this position, what progress, I ask, could the friends of temperance hope to make in their work of reform? It requires all the moral power which they can command to make headway against the depraved appetite of the drunkard, with the church and clergy *nominally* in their favor. What, then, could they do with this mighty influence openly pitted against them, and on the side of the drunkard? Would they ever dream of putting down intemperance by *political action*, so long as the land was cursed with a drunken and besotted church and priesthood, and they were themselves in full fellowship with that church and priesthood? Surely, no man in his sober senses would ever seriously entertain such an idea. Men of sense would see, at a glance, that the church and clergy were a strong and impervious rampart around the citadel of intemperance, and that the only hope of our country was in their speedy conversion or utter overthrow.

But is there any analogy between the case I have here supposed and the one under consideration? Is it true that thousands of the ministers of our country are slaveholders? Are our deacons, in countless numbers, slave-breeders and slave-traders? Do docters of divinity, and presidents of our theological seminaries, enhance their wealth by plundering cradles and trundlebeds? Do members and officers of the A. B. C. F. M. and of the A. B. S. claim their neighbors' wives and daughters, and appropriate them to their own use as chattels personal? Have presbyteries passed resolves that "the holding of slaves, so far from being a sin in the sight of God, is nowhere condemned in his holy word"? Has the General Conference of the Methodist Episcopal church publicly declared that it had "no right, wish, or intention" to abolish the infernal slave system?

Has Professor Stuart denounced the lectures of abolitionists as mere "spouting and vehemence," and boldly declared that the strong may enslave the weak, without violating the "Christian faith or the church"? And has President Fisk endorsed this doctrine, and asserted that "it will stand, because it is *Bible doctrine*"? Do those sects and local ecclesiastical bodies which adopt resolutions in favor of anti-slavery, at the same time slander and vilify the character of its firmest and most unflinching friends, because they refuse to recognize a pro-slavery church and clergy as the followers of Christ? And do they, as a body, still persist in voting for slave-claimants and pro-slavery men to fill the highest offices in the gift of the people, and that, too, against the earnest remonstrances and entreaties of the abolitionists? Truth, I regret to say, requires an affirmative answer to all these questions! The entire body of the church and clergy of the country are in Christian fellowship with slavery, that is, with those who legalize the system; while a large proportion of them are its open and unblushing advocates and apologists! Not a solitary sect in the land, of any magnitude, has espoused the anti-slavery cause. They all, without exception, stand on the side of the oppressor, and legalize his atrocities. They pass from the communion table to the ballot-box, and there deposit their votes for the man who has robbed his neighbor's cradle, to fill the highest office in the gift of the people. Not a chain has been forged,—not a fetter has been riveted on any human being in the District of Columbia, without their sanction! The question has often been put to them, Do you, the professed ministers and followers of Christ, wish the capital of your country to remain a human flesh-mart, where your Saviour may be sold, in the person of his followers, under the auction hammer? and they have as often returned an affirmative answer! And, whenever the abolitionists have sent up their petitions to Congress for the abolition of slavery, the church and clergy have sent men there, as their representatives, who have basely trampled those petitions under their feet!

But it is not in their political capacity that the influence of the church and clergy has been most prejudicial to the cause of emancipation. True, they have rivalled the infidel and nothing-arian in their support of pro-slavery parties ; and their recreancy at the ballot-box has been such as to merit the severest epithets which I have ever bestowed upon them. But in their ecclesiastical character, *they have publicly defended the slave system as an innocent and Heaven-ordained institution, and have thrown the sacred sanctions of religion around it, by introducing it into the pulpit, and to the communion table!* At the South, nearly the entire body of the clergy publicly advocate the perpetuity of slavery, and denounce the abolitionists as fanatics, incendiaries, and cut-throats ; and the churches and clergy of the North still fellowship them, and palm them off upon the world as the ministers of Christ. I know it will be said that there are exceptions to this charge ; but if there be any, I have yet to learn of them. I know not of a single ecclesiastical body in the country which has excommunicated any of its members for the crime of slaveholding, since the commencement of the anti-slavery enterprise, though most of them have cast out the true and faithful abolitionists from their communion.

I might, with great propriety, pursue these general remarks, and indulge in a somewhat severer strain ; but to understand the true character of the American church and clergy, and the full extent of their atrocities, you must hear them speak in their own language. Should I tell you the *whole* truth respecting them, and tell it in my own words, I fear you would entertain the same opinion of me that the Bramin did of his English friend, who, on a cer-

2*

tain occasion, as they were walking together along the banks of a beautiful river, admiring the richness of its scenery, *imprudently* remarked, that in his country, during the winter season, the water became so solid that an elephant could walk upon it. The Bramin replied,—" Sir, you have told me many strange and incredible things respecting your country before, yet I have always believed you to be a man of truth, but now I know you lie." So, if I tell the truth respecting the American church and clergy. I am afraid you will think me guilty of falsehood. I will therefore introduce several of the leading sects, and let them speak for themselves, through the resolves of their respective ecclesiastical bodies, and the published sentiments of their accredited ministers ; and although you may not believe me, should I tell you that they have " no wish or intention" to abolish slavery, yet you will believe them, I trust, when you hear the declaration from their own lips. I will begin with

## THE METHODIST EPISCOPAL CHURCH.

This church extends, in territory, over the whole Union, and embraces in its communion, at the present time, over 1,000,000 members, of whom probably not less than 100,000 are slaves. It comprises thirty-two Annual Conferences, from which delegates are chosen to meet in General Conference, once in four years. The church is governed by six bishops, who are elected by the General Conference, and whose duty it is to preside at the Annual Conferences ; fix the appointment of preachers ; ordain bishops, elders, and deacons ; and oversee the spiritual and temporal business of the church.

The first meeting of the General Conference, subsequent to the formation of the American Anti-Slavery Society, was in Cincinnati, in May, 1836. On the evening of the 10th of May, the Cincinnati A. S. S. held a public meeting, which was addressed by two of the members of the Conference. On the 12th of May, Rev. S. G. Roszell presented to the Conference the following preamble and resolutions :

" Whereas great excitement has pervaded this country on the subject of modern abolitionism, which is reported to have been increased in this city recently, by the unjustifiable conduct of two members of the General Conference in lecturing upon, and in favor of that agitating topic ; and whereas such a course on the part of any of its members is calculated to bring upon this body the suspicion and distrust of the community, and misrepresent its sentiments in regard to the point at issue ; and whereas, in this aspect of the case, a due regard for its own character, as well as a just concern for the interests of the church confided to its care, demand a full, decided, and unequivocal expression of the views of the General Conference in the premises ; "—Therefore,

Resolved,—

1. "By the delegates of the Annual Conference in General Conference assembled, that they disapprove, in the most unqualified sense, the conduct of the two members of the General Conference, who are reported to have lectured in this city recently upon, and in favor of modern abolitionism."

Resolved,—

2. " By the delegates of the Annual Conference in General Conference assembled,—that they are decidedly opposed to modern abolitionism, and wholly disclaim any right, wish, or intention to interfere in the civil and political relation between master and slave, as it exists in the slaveholding states of the Union."

These resolutions, after a full discussion, were adopted by the Conference—the first by a vote of 122 to 11, the last 120 to 14.

Accompanying these resolutions, as they went forth to the world to " define the position" of the Methodist Episcopal church on the great question which is now agitating the land, was a pastoral address to the churches, which contains the following passages :

" These facts, which are only mentioned here as a reason for the friendly admonition which we wish to give you, constrain us, as your pastors, who are called to watch over your souls, as they must give account, to exhort you to *abstain from all abolition movements and associations*, and to refrain from patronizing any of their publications. &c.

" From every view of the subject which we have been able to take, and from the most calm and dispassionate survey of the whole ground, we have come to the conclusion, that the only safe, scriptural, and prudent way for us, both as ministers and people, to take, is *wholly to refrain from this agitating subject*," &c.

Such was the language of the representative body of the Methodist Episcopal church on the great question of emancipation in 1836. They here declare, emphatically, that they have no " *wish* or *intention* to interfere in the civil and political relation between master and slave," and exhort their brethren to " abstain from all abolition movements and associations," and " wholly to refrain from this agitating subject"! And what could a conclave of demons in hell have said more ? Surely no *other* banditti on earth would have gone so far—not in hypocrisy, at least, if they had in cold-blooded barbarity. Mark the language of the reverend scoundrels. They have no " *wish* or *intention* " to abolish the infernal slave system! Every circumstance of the scene contributes to heighten their guilt. They claim to be ambassadors of Christ, assembled for the purpose of extending his kingdom on the earth,—before them lie two millions of their countrymen, ground into the very dust beneath "a bondage, one hour of which is fraught with more misery than ages of that which our fathers rose in rebellion to oppose;" and yet they have " no *wish* or *intention* to interfere with their civil and political relations"! These hapless victims of republican despotism are prohibited by law from learning the letters of the alphabet, and, of course, from reading the Bible ; and as a necessary consequence of their condition as chattels, they are deprived of the institution of marriage, and doomed to a life of universal prostitution and concubinage— and yet they have " no *wish* or *intention* to interfere with their civil and political relations"! A million of American women are daily thrown into the market, and offered for sale for purposes of prostitution, to any person of sufficient wealth to command their price—and yet they have " no *wish* or *intention* to interfere with their civil and political relations "! They see before them men and women, many of them members of their own church, chained together by dozens and scores, handcuffed, and driven from their homes, and all that is dear to them on earth, to a distant market, and there sold with the meanest brutes—and yet they have " no *wish* or *intention* to interfere with their civil and political relations"! They look abroad over the country, and behold the hundreds of mothers who are daily robbed of their darling babes, and witness the keen anguish and perfect desperation to which they are often driven by the strength of maternal affection—and yet they have "no *wish* or *intention* to interfere with their civil and political relations "! No, they have not one solitary word of consolation for the poor, heart-broken, despairing slave! They have "*no wish* " to see him free! So they tell us. The clank of the chain, and the crack of the driver's whip, are music to their ears! They cannot even pray that this nefarious system may come to an end, for "*they are decidedly opposed to modern abolitionism.*" Not less so, doubtless, than Beelzebub himself. They *prefer* the continuance of slavery! And not content with merely passing by their robbed and bleeding countrymen, like the priest and Levite of old, and leaving them to the charities of others, they must turn aside from their *pious* calling to give a dagger-thrust at the reputation of those who are kindly binding up their wounds!

The next meeting of this body was in Baltimore, in 1840. It was to be hoped that the rising spirit of liberty which was now agitating the country, and opening the eyes of thousands to the wrongs of our enslaved countrymen, would reach the ministry of the Methodist church, and in some degree, at least, soften their obdurate hearts. But the action of this Conference shows that the preaching of the truth, so far as they were concerned, had only proved " a savor of death unto death." Instead of lightening the burdens of the previous Conference, their *little finger* was thicker than their predecessors' loins. The Conference of 1836 had chastised the slaves and their advocates with whips, but they chastised them with scorpions Up to this date, the slaves in this church had, nominally at least, enjoyed that last privilege of the oppressed, the right of complaint. But, for reasons to which I shall hereafter refer, this sacred right was now wrested from them, and all recognition of their manhood totally annihilated at one fell swoop, by the adoption of the following resolution, which was presented by the Rev. Dr. A. G. Few, of Georgia :

Resolved,—
" That it is inexpedient and unjustifiable for any preacher to permit colored persons to give testimony against white persons, in any state where they are denied that privilege by law."

By this rule, which is now a part of the discipline of the church, more than 80,000 of its colored members are denied the right to testify against a *white* brother or sister in any case whatsoever. No matter what the crime may be, or how aggravating the circumstances. The reverend mover of the resolution can now violate the chastity of the colored members of his church with entire impunity. He is no longer in any danger of being censured and silenced by his more fortunate brethren, as the *late* Rev. Dr. Fay was. Should he unfortunately be " *overtaken in a fault*," the church has " provided a way of escape." And an ample provision it is, even for the *chiefest* of sinners. Neither the reverend doctor, nor any of his coadjutors, could desire greater liberty—or *privileges*, as they might term it. The lips of their victims and her friends are now hermetically sealed up, both in the church and in the civil tribunals. The aggrieved party can now obtain no redress, however aggravated the offence. The state has declared her body to be the *property* of her white brother ; and the church has decided that it will entertain none of her complaints, whatever use he may make of it. What more could even the *clergy* ask ? But I forbear.

The course of the faithless miscreants who adopted this and the preceding resolutions, was acquiesced in by *all* the local Conferences, and cordially approved by most of them, and by nearly all the distinguished and influential ministers in the denomination.

In support of the position assumed by the General Conference, the Ohio Annual Conference

Resolved,—

"That those brethren of the North, who *resist the abolition movements* with firmness and moderation, are the true friends of the church, to the slaves of the South, and to the constitution of our common country," etc.

The New York Annual Conference

Resolved,—

1. "That this Conference fully concur in the advice of the late General Conference, as expressed in their Pastoral Address.

2. "That we disapprove of the members of this Conference patronizing, or in any way giving countenance to a paper called 'Zion's Watchman,' because, in our opinion it tends to disturb the peace and harmony of the body, by sowing dissension in the church."

Resolved,—

3. "That although we do not condemn any man, or withhold our suffrages from him on account of his *opinions* merely, in reference to the subject of abolitionism, yet we are decidedly of the opinion that none ought to be elected to the office of deacon or elder in our church, unless he give a pledge to the Conference, that he will refrain from agitating the church with discussions on this subject."

The Georgia Annual Conference

Resolved *unanimously*,—

1. "That it is the sense of the Georgia Annual Conference, that slavery, as it exists in the United States, *is not a moral evil*."

Resolved,—

2. "That we view *slavery* as a civil and domestic institution, and one with which, as ministers of Christ, we have nothing to do, further than to ameliorate the condition of the slave, by endeavoring to impart to him and his master the benign influence of the religion of Christ, and aiding both on their way to heaven."

Which religion in the opinion of the Methodist Episcopal church, is not opposed to the perpetuity of slavery; but allows one member of the church to claim and use another's *wife* as his property, and to appropriate her to such use as *he* may deem proper or desirable, the enslaved woman having no right to enter and substantiate a complaint against her master before the church! This is Methodism! This is the religion which the Methodist clergy "*impart*" to the poor, heart-broken slave, and to his inhuman master. This, too, is the religion which they "*impart*" to their poor deluded vassals at the North. Bear with me while I present a few more specimens of it from the lips of its most distinguished advocates.

Rev. E. D. Simons, professor in Macon College:

"These extracts from HOLY WRIT UNEQUIVOCALLY ASSERT THE RIGHT OF PROPERTY IN SLAVES, together with the usual incidents of that right; such as the power of acquisition and disposition in various ways, according to municipal regulations. The right to buy and sell, and to transmit to children by the way of inheritance, is clearly stated. The only restriction on the subject is in reference to the *market*, in which slaves or bond men were to be purchased.

"Upon the whole, then, whether we consult the Jewish polity instituted by God himself, or the uniform opinion and practice of mankind in all ages of the world, or the injunctions of the New Testament and the moral law, we are brought to the conclusion that slavery is not immoral.

"Having established the point that the first African slaves were legally brought into bondage, the right to detain their children in bondage, follows as an indispensable consequence.

"Thus we see that the slavery which exists in America was *founded in right.*"

Rev. Wilbur Fisk, D. D., late president of the Wesleyan University, Connecticut:

"The relation of master and servant may, and *does, in many cases,* exist under such circumstances, as frees the master from the just charge and guilt of immorality. .

"The general rule of Christianity *not only permits,* but, in supposable circumstances, *enjoins a continuance of the master's authority.*

"The New Testament enjoins obedience upon the slave as an obligation *due* to a present *rightful* authority."

Elijah Hedding, D. D., one of the six Methodist bishops:

"The right to hold a slave is founded on this rule: 'Therefore, all things whatsoever ye would that men should do to you, do ye even so unto them; for this is the law and the prophets.'"

Rev. William Winans, of Mississippi, in the General Conference, in 1836:

"He was not born in a slave state—he was a Pennsylvanian by birth. He had been brought up to believe a slaveholder as great a villain as a horse-thief; but he had gone to the South, and long residence there had changed his views; he had become a slaveholder *on principle.*" * * * "Though a slaveholder himself, no abolitionist felt more sympathy for the slave than he did—none had rejoiced more in the hope of a coming period, when the print of a slave's foot would not be seen on the soil." * * * "It was important to the interests of slaves, and in view of the question of slavery, that there be Christians who were slaveholders. Christian ministers should be slaveholders, and diffused throughout the South. Yes, sir, Presbyterians, Baptists, Methodists, should be slaveholders:—yes, he repeated it boldly—there should be members, and *deacons*, and ELDERS, and BISHOPS, too, who were slaveholders."

Rev. J. C. Postell, Orangeburg, South Carolina, in an address at a public meeting called for the purpose of opposing abolition:

"From what has been premised the following conclusions result: 1. That slavery is a judicial visitation. 2. *That it is not a moral evil.* 3. *That it is supported by the Bible.* 4. It has existed in all ages.

"It is not a moral evil. The fact, that slavery is of DIVINE APPOINTMENT, would be proof enough with the Christian that it cannot be a moral evil." * * * "So far from being a moral evil, *it is a merciful visitation.* If slavery was either the invention of man, or a moral evil, it is logical to conclude, the power to create has the power to destroy. Why, then, has it existed? And why does it now exist amid all the power of legislation in state and church, and the clamor of abolitionists? *It is the Lord's* DOINGS, AND IT IS MARVELLOUS IN OUR EYES; and had it not been for the best, God alone, who is able, long since would have overruled it. IT IS BY DIVINE APPOINTMENT."

The same individual to the editor of *Zion's Watchman:*

"To La Roy Sunderland, &c.
"Did you calculate to misrepresent the Methodist discipline, and say it supported abolitionism, when the General Conference, in their late resolutions, denounced it as a *libel on truth.* '*O full of all subtlety, thou child of the devil!*' all *liars*, saith the sacred volume, shall have their part in the lake of fire and brimstone.

"I can only give one reason why you have not been indicted for a libel. The law says, 'The greater the truth the greater the libel;' and as your paper has no such ingredient, it is construed but a small matter. But if you desire to educate the slaves, I will tell you how to raise the money, without editing *Zion's Watchman.* You and old Arthur Tappan come out to the South this winter, and they will raise one hundred thousand dollars for you. New Orleans itself will be pledged for it. Desiring no further acquaintance with you, and never expecting to see you but once in time or eternity, that is, at the judgment, I subscribe myself, the friend of the Bible, and the opposer of abolitionists.

"J. C. POSTELL,
"Orangeburg, July 21st, 1836."

Rev. Geo. W. Langhorne, of North Carolina, to the editor of *Zion's Herald:*

"I, sir, would as soon be found in the ranks of a banditti, as numbered with Arthur Tappan and his wanton coadjutors. Nothing is more appalling to my feelings as a man, contrary to my principles as a Christian, and *repugnant* to my soul as a *minister*, than the insidious proceedings of such men.

"If you have not resigned your credentials as a minister of the Methodist Episcopal church, I really think that, as an *honest* man, you should now do it. In your ordination vows you solemnly promised to be obedient to those who have rule over you; and since they (the General Conference) have spoken, and that distinctly, too, on this subject, and disapprobate your conduct, I conceive you are bound to submit to their authority, or leave the church."

Rev. Mr. Crawder, of Virginia, in the General Conference, 1840:

"Slavery is not only countenanced, permitted, and regulated, by the Bible, but it was positively *instituted* by GOD HIMSELF—he has in so many words ENJOINED it."

Such is the present ecclesiastical position of the Methodist Episcopal church, in relation to the system which John Wesley denounced as the sum of all villanies, and which, as I have clearly shown, no person can support or countenance, directly or indirectly, without thereby becoming a *felon* of the most odious and criminal character. "Nearly one half of the ministers," in the eleven states of the Union, "hold slaves and trade in them"— that is, they claim their neighbors' wives, rob *cradles* and *trundle-beds*, and sell their own church members for purposes of prostitution (if the purchaser choose to put them to that use); and the church, meanwhile, through its highest tribunal, by a vote of 120 to 14, declares itself "*decidedly opposed*" to the abolition of this monstrous wickedness, and asserts that it has "no *right, wish, or intention* to interfere" with it; and one of the six bishops, and he a Northern man, the Rev. Elijah Hedding, D. D., tells us that "the right to hold slaves"—that is, to claim his neighbors' wife and daughters as his property, and to *use* them as such—"is founded on the rule, 'Therefore all things whatsoever ye would that others should do to you, do ye even so to them!'!" Is not this church, then, a "Brotherhood of Thieves"? Is it not, rather, a *conclave of incarnate fiends*, whose influence is as much more corrupting to the morals of the community than the influence of the theatre, as its doctrines are more *damnable?* For one, much as I deprecate the erection of a theatre, I deprecate the erection of a Methodist meeting-house *more!* The stage does not teach my neighbors that the New Testament allows them to enslave my wife and children; but the Methodist pulpit *does!* I know not in what light you view this subject, but for myself I regard every *intelligent* communicant in the Methodist church as more guilty and infamous, in the sight of God, than the common prostitute, the pickpocket, or the assassin; and I cannot associate with him on any other terms of intercourse than those which I stipulate for these infamous characters.

But the Methodists are not sinners above all the sects in the land. All the other large denominations are of a kindred character, as will appear from an examination of their ecclesiastical history, and the sentiments of their most distinguished ministers. They all legalize slavery, and most of them, as we shall see, own slaves, and publicly vindicate the system, or are silent as to its wrongs. This is specially true of

## THE PRESBYTERIAN AND CONGREGATIONAL CHURCH.

The Presbyterians and orthodox Congregationalists of the United States, numbering in all about 600,000 communicants, are virtually one sect, or denomination; their only difference being about church government. On all other points of religious faith, *slavery* not excepted, they are agreed. They are all in Christian fellowship with each other; and are connected together by Associations, Presbyteries, Synods, and General Assemblies. They are united in their missionary operations; their ministers intermingle on exchanges and parochial settlements; their communion table is common; and they recommend and receive members from one to the other without any change of faith. And to make the fellowship more complete, and the connection more perfect, the General Association of the Congregationalists, in all the New England States, where the Congregational church is mainly located, send delegates to the General Assembly of the Presbyterian church and receive their delegates in return. In 1838, the General Assembly separated on some unimportant points of doctrine; but the *denomination* is still *one* and *undivided;* and the separation was nothing more than the cleaving of air, which closes immediately behind the intersecting instrument. Hence, connected as all the local churches are with the general body, no person can unite with any one of them without being thereby brought into fellowship with the whole; for there is no local church in the country, of which I have any knowledge, which is disconnected from the main body; and it is not material whether we fellowship slave-claimants directly, or fellowship those who are in fellowship with them. In either case, the chain which binds us to slavery being unbroken, we partake of its sins, and must receive of its plagues.

Now, there are in this church a large number of clergymen, men of great influence with the denomination, who gain their subsistence by preaching sermons, making prayers, and stealing babes! These "spiritual guides" of the Presbyterian church, like their brethren of the Methodist church, claim their neighbors' wives and daughters, and appropriate them to their own use. They tell us that these women are *theirs*—that they *own* them. Of course, if they own them, they can do what they *will* with their own; and what a clergyman would be likely to do with his own women—women over whom he not only possessed unlimited power, but to whose bodies he had a divine right—those can best judge who are acquainted with the records of that department of the Female Moral Reform Society, which treats of the licentiousness of the clergy. And what is done by the leaders is also done by the people. Thousands of the lay members of this church are slave-breeders, whose chief or only source of income is the sale of human flesh! Their plantations are stocked with women, members, in part, of the same church, whom they term BREEDERS; and not a few of them are engaged on an extensive scale, in raising *boys* and *girls* from these *breeders*, for the rice and cotton fields of the far South; as the Berkshire farmers raise cattle and horses for Brighton market!!

But the clergy of this genteel and influential sect have not been content with merely upholding slavery by the force of their example. Like faithful sentinels on its watch-towers, they were the first to descry the *dangers* of abolition; and from the commencement of the anti-slavery enterprise, they have been among the most active and energetic in arousing the people to determined and obstinate resistance. No sect in the land has done more to perpetuate slavery than this. Its deliberate and coldblooded sanction and approval of the slave-system, and its *murderous* appeal to the mob to put a stop to the progress of free principles by Lynch law, is enough to make one's blood curdle in his veins!—But hear them in their own words, recollecting, meanwhile, that they claim to be the ministers of Christ, and that before them lie 2,700,000 wretched slaves, imploring relief at their hands. Here is their answer to the demand of crushed humanity for the recognition of its inalienable rights.

Charleston Union Presbytery:

Resolved,—
"That in the opinion of this Presbytery, the holding of slaves, *so far from being a sin in the sight of God, is nowhere condemned in his holy word*—that it is in accordance with the example, or consistent with the precepts, of patriarchs, apostles, and prophets, and that it is compatible with the most fraternal regard to the best good of those servants whom God may have committed to our charge."

Harmony Presbytery, South Carolina:

Resolved, unanimously,—
"1. That, as the kingdom of our Lord is not of this world, his church, as such, has no right to abolish, alter, or affect any institution or ordinance of men, political and civil merely, &c.
"2. That slavery has existed from the days of those good old slaveholders and patriarchs, Abraham, Isaac, and Jacob (who are now in the kingdom of heaven), to the time when the apostle Paul sent a runaway slave home to his master Philemon, and wrote a Christian and fraternal epistle to this slaveholder, which we find still stands in the canons of the Scriptures; and that slavery has existed ever since the days of the apostle, and does now exist.
"3. That, as the relative duties of master and slave are taught in the Scriptures, in the same manner as those of parent and child, and husband and wife, *the existence of slavery itself is not opposed to the will of God;* and whosoever has a conscience too tender to recognize this relation as lawful, is 'righteous overmuch,' is 'wise above what is written,' and has submitted his neck to the yoke of man, sacrificed his Christian liberty of conscience, and leaves the infallible word of God for the fancies and doctrines of men."

Synod of South Carolina and Georgia:

Resolved, unanimously [Dec., 1834,]—
"That, in the opinion of this Synod, Abolition Societies, and the principles upon which they are founded, in the United States, are inconsistent with the interests of the slaves, the rights of the holders, and the great principles of our political institutions."

Rev. Robert N. Anderson, Virginia:

"To the Sessions of the Presbyterian Congregations within the Bounds of West Hanover Presbytery:

"At the approaching stated meeting of our Presbytery, I design to offer a preamble and string of resolutions on the subject of the use of wine in the Lord's supper ; and also *a preamble and a string of resolutions on the subject of the treasonable and abominably wicked interference of the Northern and Eastern fanatics with our political and civil rights, our property, and our domestic concerns. I myself, dear brethren, have no reason to doubt the perfect soundness of all my clerical brethren of this Presbytery on these subjects.* But you are fully aware that the present state of things loudly and imperiously calls for an expression of their views on these subjects, and particularly on abolitionism, by all church bodies at the South. You are aware also, that our clergy, whether with or without reason, are more suspected by the public than are the clergy of other denominations. Now, dear Christian brethren, I humbly express it as my earnest wish, that you quit yourselves like men ; that every congregation send up both to the Presbytery and to the Synod the ablest elder it has. The times— rely upon it—the times demand it. *If there be any stray goat of a minister among us, tainted with the blood-hound principles of abolitionism, let him be ferreted out, silenced, excommunicated, and left to the public to dispose of him in other respects.*
" Your affectionate brother in the Lord,
"ROBERT N. ANDERSON."

Rev. Thomas S. Witherspoon, of Alabama, to the editor of the *Emancipator:*

"I draw my warrant from the Scriptures of the Old and New Testament, to hold the slave in bondage. The principle of holding the heathen in bondage is recognized by God." * * * *
" When the tardy process of law is too long in redressing our grievances, we of the South have adopted the summary remedy of Judge Lynch—and really I think it is one of the most wholesome and salutary remedies for the malady of Northern fanaticism that can be applied, and no doubt my worthy friend, the editor of the *Emancipator and Human Rights,* would feel the better of its enforcement, provided he had a Southern administrator. I go to the Bible for my warrant in all moral matters." * * *
" Let your emissaries dare venture to cross the Potomac, and I cannot promise you that their fate will be less than Haman's. Then beware how you goad an insulted but magnanimous people to deeds of desperation."

Rev. Wm. S. Plummer, D. D., Virginia :

[To the Chairman of a Committee of Correspondence, appointed by the citizens of Richmond, to oppose the progress of anti-slavery principles at the South.]

" I have carefully watched the matter from its earliest existence, and everything I have seen and heard of its character, both from its patrons and its enemies, has confirmed me, beyond repentance, in the belief that, let the character of abolitionists be what it may in the sight of the Judge of all the earth, this is the most meddlesome, impudent, reckless, fierce, and wicked excitement I ever saw. I am willing at any time that the *world* should know that such are my views. A few things are perfectly clear to my mind.

" 1st. The more speedy, united, firm, and solemnly resolute, but temperate, the expression of public opinion on this subject in the whole South, the better it will be for the North, for slaveholders, and generally for the slaves.

" 2d. If abolitionists will set the country in a blaze, *it is but fair that they should have the first warming at the fire.*"

\* \* \* \* \* \* \* \* \* \*

" Lastly. Abolitionists are, like infidels, wholly unaddicted to martyrdom for opinion's sake. Let them understand that they *will be caught,* if they come among us, and they will take good heed to keep out of our way. There is not one man among them who has any more idea of shedding his blood in this cause, than he has of making war on the Grand Turk. Their universal spirit is to stand off, and growl and bark at men and institutions, without daring to march for one moment into their midst, and attack them with apostolic fearlessness.

" With sentiments of great respect, I remain yours, &c.,
" WM. S. PLUMMER."

I know of no language in the vocabulary which is adequate to express the abhorrence, which must be felt by every untainted mind towards the authors of the atrocious sentiments contained in the three last documents, and also towards the church and denomination that will sustain them, and palm them upon the world as ministers of Christ. What! has it come to this, that pastors of churches and doctors of divinity can not only *steal their neighbors' wives*, without fear of reproach, but openly advocate LYNCH LAW, and that, too, in its most frightful shape, for the suppression of free discussion? William S. Plummer is not only a doctor of divinity, but one of the most popular ministers in all the South. He is at the head of the New School in the Presbyterian church, and is a prominent member of the A. B. C. F. M. And yet his letter is a direct appeal to the mob to BURN US ALIVE, if we go among them! He calls upon the citizens of Richmond to react the Vicksburg tragedy!—to " *catch* " the abolitionists, and give them a "*warming at the fire*"! And this call comes to them from the pulpit, and endorsed by every Presbyterian and Congregationalist in the land, for they all recognize William S. Plummer as a Christian minister! These three men are *execrable murderers*, if Christ's definition of murder be the true one; and yet they are of no doubtful standing in the Presbyterian church! These are the men whose delegates are annually received by every Congregational Association in New England!

Rev. Moses Stuart, professor in Andover Theological Seminary, Massachusetts:

[To Rev. Wilbur Fisk, D. D., president of the Wesleyan University, Connecticut].

"ANDOVER, 10th April, 1837.

"Rev. and dear sir,—Yours is before me. A sickness of three months' standing (typhus fever), in which I have just escaped death, and which still confines me to my house, renders it impossible for me to answer your letter at large.

"1. The precepts of the New Testament respecting the demeanor of slaves and their masters, beyond all question, recognize the existence of slavery. The masters are in part 'believing masters,' so that a precept to them, how they are to behave as *masters*, recognizes that the relation may still exist, *salva fide et salva ecclesia*(without violating the Christian faith or the church). Otherwise, Paul had nothing to do but to cut the band asunder at once. He could not lawfully and properly temporize with a *malum in se* (that which is in itself sin).

"If any one doubts, let him take the case of Paul's sending Onesimus back to Philemon, with an apology for his running away, and sending him back to be his servant for life. The relation did exist, may exist. The *abuse* of it is the essential and fundamental wrong. Not that the theory of slavery is in itself right. No; 'Love thy neighbor as thyself,' 'Do unto others that which ye would that others should do unto you,' decide against this. But the relation once constituted and continued, is not such a *malum in se* as calls for immediate and violent disruption, at all hazard. So Paul did not counsel."

\*     \*     \*     \*     \*     \*     \*     \*

"After all the spouting and vehemence on this subject, which have been exhibited, the *good old book* remains the same—[that is, in favor of slavery.] Paul's conduct and advice are still safe guides. Paul knew well that Christianity would ultimately destroy slavery, as it certainly will. He knew, too that it would destroy monarchy and aristocracy from the earth; for it is fundamentally a doctrine of *true liberty and equality*. Yet Paul did not expect slavery and monarchy to be ousted in a day ; and gave precepts to Christians respecting their demeanor *ad interim.*

"With sincere and fraternal regard,

"Your friend and brother,

"M. STUART."

Rev. Wilbur Fisk, D. D. to a friend :

"This, sir [referring to the preceding letter], is doctrine that will stand, because it is *Bible doctrine.* The abolitionists, then, are on the wrong course. They have travelled out of their record ; and if they would succeed, they must take a different position, and approach the subject in a different manner.

"Respectfully yours, W. FISK."

There are several things in this letter, and the endorsement by Dr. Fisk, which deserve particular attention.

1. The writer and endorser, at the time of its publication, were both engaged in fitting young men for the ministry, and the former still occupies the same responsible station.

2. They were elected to their respective offices by New England ministers ; and no objection has ever been made to their retaining their offices on account of their opinions on slavery. They may, therefore, be considered as the representatives of the New England clergy, on the question of slavery.

3. The opinions of no clergymen in the country have greater weight, in their respective sects, than those of Professor Stuart and President Fisk.

4. Both are united in opposing emancipation ; and they are equally responsible for all the sentiments and statements contained in this letter.

5. This letter is as full and complete a recognition of slavery as any slave-claimant in the land could desire. It expressly says " that the relation may exist ;" that is, one man may claim and use another's wife and children as his property " without violating the Christian faith or the church" ! "Slavery," it adds, "did exist, *may* exist ! The *abuse* of it is the essential and fundamental wrong" ! That is, to convert a man into an article of merchandise, and exercise unlimited power over him, is not sinful ; but whipping him unnecessarily may be. This is the doctrine of the letter.

6. To maintain this doctrine, the letter states a gross and palpable *falsehood.* It says that Paul sent Onesimus back to Philemon " to be his *servant* for life." Nothing could be farther from the truth than this statement. Had the reverend authors of it said that Jesus himself was a slaveholder, they would not have been guilty of a greater libel or more horrible blasphemy !

Paul's language to Philemon cannot possibly be misunderstood. He calls Onesimus his *son*, and tells Philemon to receive him as his " *own bowels ;*" that is, as his own offspring. He tells him expressly to receive him " *not now as a servant, but above a servant, a brother beloved, both in the flesh and in the Lord.*" He tells him still further,—" *Receive him as myself;*" that is, as you would the great Apostle to the Gentiles ; and he adds,—" If he oweth thee aught, put that on my account; I will repay it." And he remarks, in apology for sending back Onesimus, that he had perfect confidence in Philemon, that he would do even more for him than he had asked. And yet, with this plain and unequivocal statement before them, these distinguished biblical scholars have the audacity to tell us, that Paul sent Onesimus back " to be a *servant* for life !" Alas ! to what lengths slave-claimants and their abettors will go, in supporting their horrible system ! They will beat, imprison, and burn abolitionists, and lie, and blaspheme the God of Heaven, in its defence ! We have here, in immediate connection, five clergymen, three of them publicly advocating lynch law ; and the remaining two publishing to the world the most glaring and libellous falsehoods, for the purpose of destroying the remnant of sympathy which is still felt for the helpless victims of their power !

## THE GENERAL ASSEMBLIES, OLD AND NEW SCHOOL.

The course pursued by these bodies on the subject of slavery is a *fac simile* of that adopted by the United States Congress. They have never taken any action on the subject in favor of emancipation, and have generally succeeded in preventing a full discussion of it; although it has at times crept in, and caused them no little trouble. This, however, is nothing more than was to be expected of bodies composed mainly of man-stealers, and those who legalize man-stealing. Indeed, ecclesiastical action against slavery, while their character remains what it now is, is not to be desired.

The first thing which they can do for the slave, is to " repent and be converted," and become abolitionists indeed. Till then, the adoption of resolutions against slavery would only render them more dangerous and formidable enemies of the cause of freedom, since it would enable them the more effectually to deceive and beguile many of its honest, but less discerning, friends.

I might go into an extended narration of their proceedings, but they are too barren of interest to warrant the trouble. Suffice it to say, that while they refused, at their late meetings, to pass
3

any censure on slaveholding, the old school pronounced a man guilty of " INCEST," and deposed him from the ministry, for marrying the sister of his deceased wife ; and the new bore a formal and very solemn testimony against dancing, as a sin not to be tolerated in the church!

What would be thought of the Bey of Tunis, or the Sultan, should he enact a law prohibiting dancing in his dominions, as a crime, and at the same time allow one class of his subjects to enslave and imbrute another, or sell them in the market,—as the executors of the late Rev. Dr. Furman, president of the Baptist Triennial Convention, recently sold twenty-seven native Americans under the hammer of the auctioneer, with his "theological library, two mules, one horse, and an old wagon"? Such a demonstration of barbarism in a Mahometan prince would excite the astonishment and indignation of all Christendom. But in Christian " *divines*" it is all well enough. At least, the great body of the people think so. Coming as it does from their priests, it is to them all gospel.

But it is due to the Bey of Tunis (the man whom our American clergy look upon as a heathen, and to whom they are now sending missionaries), to say, in this connection, that he has not only not enacted a law against the very harmless amusement of dancing (David and the old prophets danced), but that he has enacted a law prohibiting slaveholding in his dominions. Let the clergy of our country read the following letter from him to the British residents at Gibraltar If it does not raise a blush upon their cheeks, it will be because they are lost to all sense of shame :

*Translation.*

" Praise be to God !

" From the servant of God, Musheer Ahmed Bashaw Bey, Sovereign Prince of the dominions of Tunis, to the perfectly honored Englishmen, united together for the amelioration of the human race.—May God honor them !

" We have received the letter which you have forwarded to us, by the honored and reverend Richardson, congratulating us upon the measures * that we have adopted for the glory of mankind, to *distinguish them from the brute creation.*

" Your letter has filled us with joy and satisfaction.

" May God aid us in our efforts—may he enable us to accomplish the objects of our hopes—and may he accept this our work !

" May you live continually under the protection of God Almighty !

" Given at Tunis, 26th day Elhojah, 1257. [7th Feb., 1842.]"

---

* The abolition of slavery throughout his dominions.

# THE BAPTIST CHURCH.

This church contains nearly 1,000,000 members, not far from 100,000 of whom are in slavery, and many of them the goods and chattels of their own ministers, and brethren. In territory, it embraces the whole Union; but its members are most numerous at the South. The different congregations or churches are independent of each other in regard to ecclesiastical jurisdiction; but they are all united in one body, through their state and other local associations, and a General Convention, which meets once in three years, and under whose direction the foreign missionary operations of the church are carried on. Besides the General Convention, there is also a Baptist Home Mission Society, and an American and Foreign Bible Society, in which all the different sections of the country are represented, and through which the bond of union and fellowship between the local churches is strengthened, and rendered more apparent to the world.

The communion table of each of the churches is free to all the others, except in a few cases where resolutions have been adopted, excluding slaveholders (slave-claimants); but these churches invite to their table those who commune with Southern man-stealers, so that their connection with them is unbroken. No church has yet severed itself from the slaveholding body; and hence all who are connected with any one of them, are members of that body, and responsible for its acts; nor is there any essential difference in the moral condition of the different members, for the same blood which flows about the heart circulates into the most distant extremity of every limb. No church has espoused the anti-slavery cause in opposition to the body, and demanded its division. In this regard the North and South are *essentially* alike. In both, slavery finds warm friends and firm supporters. In both, there are also those who desire its abolition, but whose desires are not sufficiently strong to induce them to separate from a slaveholding church. They love their church organization, corrupt as it is, better than they love the cause of the bleeding slave. Hence they cling to it, and oppose the genuine abolitionists, who go for entire separation from slave-breeders and their Northern abettors.

Soon after the last Triennial Convention, a Provisional Foreign Mission Committee was appointed by the disaffected Baptist ministers of the New Organization, for the ostensible purpose of carrying on a system of missionary operations among the heathen, disconnected with slavery; but it proved to be a mere *trick* of the clergy, to quiet the anti-slavery agitation. All the movers of it **are**, to this day, in full fellowship with the Baptist church or denomination, as a Christian body ; and that church is made up, mainly, of slave-claimants and those who legalize slavery. And besides, a large sum of money that was raised from abolitionists, on condition that it should not be mingled with the blood-stained contributions of the South, was appropriated to the use of the old man-stealing board, as will appear from the following resolution, unanimously adopted at the first, or an early meeting of the Provisional Foreign Mission Committee :—

" Whereas the Foreign Mission Board have recently sustained a heavy loss by the failure of their banker at Calcutta, and thus appropriated supplies are cut off from the missionaries in Asia : Therefore,
" Resolved,—
" That the treasurer of this committee be instructed to forward, as soon as possible, five hundred dollars, from funds now in the treasury, to the relief of the missionaries, to be expended under the direction of Dr. Judson and Mr. Vinton.
"Simon G. Shipley, Chairman.
" Charles W. Dennison, Recording Secretary."

A second missionary association has recently been formed by a portion of the same disaffected members, called the American and Foreign Baptist Missionary Society ; but it is only another limb of the old man-stealing Baptist body. The leaders in it are still in Christian fellowship with Drs Sharp, Bolles, and Wayland, and Hon. Richard Fletcher, all of whom are officers of the old board ; and also with the Baptists generally of the North, who legalize slavery. The organization of these new missionary associations is only a *family quarrel*, and not a division in the family. But the case is one which demands separation, like that which took place in the Congregational church when a portion of it embraced the Unitarian faith.

The last General Convention of the Baptist church was characterized by base servility to the slave power, and utter recreancy to every principle of Christianity. The North and South there met together in loving fellowship, to advance the kingdom of the Redeemer. Every section of the church was fully represented. The slave-claimant, the Northern apologist of slavery, and the New Organizationist, were all there, and sat down together. They took the object of their meeting into "*prayerful consideration*," and invoked the divine blessing upon it. But— O, tell it not in Algiers !—their first act was to choose a THIEF to preside over their deliberations. Subsequently, another thief was selected to preach the sermon ; and yet another to make the prayer preparatory to the election of the Missionary Board; and he, doubtless, prayed to the God of thieves; for their next act was to drop the venerable Elon Galusha from the board, and elect a fourth thief to fill his place! And to close the *farce* they united over the communion table in singing the hymn beginning with the following lines :—

> " Lo, what an entertaining sight
> Are brethren who agree !"

Such was the character of the last Triennial Convention. And yet the New-Organized Baptist ministers, who had separated from the American Anti-Slavery Society because women were allowed to stand upon its platform, saw no occasion to withdraw from it. They could participate in a Baptist Convention whose president was a man-stealing doctor of divinity ; but they could not remain in an *anti-slavery* meeting, where women were permitted to speak. Alas, how true it is that a sectarian cannot be an *honest man !* But I am consuming too much time with my own remarks. I will let the Baptists speak for themselves. They can tell their own story better than I can tell it.

Rev. Wm. H. Brisbane, corresponding secretary of the American and Foreign Baptist Missionary Society (formerly a slave-owner) :—

"As a body, the Baptists of this country are still united in supporting, directly or indirectly, slavery and slave-trading, and, by consequence, all of its terrible evils. Baptists who have no slaves themselves are in intimate communion with those who have them. A very considerable proportion of Baptist ministers are slaveholders, and yet they have free access to the pulpits in almost every part of our common country ; yea, they administer, oftentimes by invitation of those who possess no slaves, the sacred elements of the Lord's supper. In the Baptist General Convention, for the thirty years of its organization, slaveholders and non-slaveholders have met in common fellowship. Its presidents have, for the most part, been slaveholders."

Rev. Lucius Bolles, d. d., corresponding secretary of the American Baptist Board of Foreign Missions :—

"There is a pleasing degree of union among the multiplying thousands of Baptists throughout the land. Brethren from all parts of the country meet in one general convention, and coöperate in sending the gospel to the heathen. *Our Southern brethren are liberal and zealous in the promotion of every holy enterprise for the extension of the gospel. They are generally, both ministers and people, slaveholders.*"

The Baptist man-thieves of the South are *liberal* and *zealous* in the promotion of every HOLY enterprise, forsooth! ! So says a leading D. D. of the Baptist church of the North. And he tell us, further, that there is a pleasing degree of *union* between these man-stealers and the multiplying thousands of Baptists throughout the land! This is doubtless true; but to *whom* is this union pleasing? Not, surely, to the despairing *slave*; nor to God, who can himself, of course, have no possible union with thieves, although they may be very good Baptists and Baptist ministers. But it is pleasing to the slave-master, and to the Baptist clergy generally; and it is doubtless pleasing to *their* father. Slavery is greatly strengthened by it; and whatever strengthens that institution, cannot be otherwise than pleasing to him.

Rev. W. B. Johnson. D. D., of South Carolina, president of the last General Convention :—

" When, in any country, slavery has become a part of its set-tled policy, the inhabitants, even Christians, *may hold slaves with-out crime.*"

Rev. Daniel Sharp, Massachusetts, to Rev. Otis Smith:

*" In regard to church action in the case* I consider it both *inex-pedient and unscriptural. There were, undoubtedly, both slave-holders and slaves in the primitive churches. I, therefore, for one, do not feel myself at liberty to make conditions of communion which neither Christ nor his apostles made. I do not consider myself wiser or better than they were.* Nor have I yet made such prog-ress in knowledge as to believe that a good end sanctifies *unjusti-fiable means.* I believe that *a majority of the wisest and best men* at the North hold to these sentiments. But if I stood alone, here I shall remain immovable, unless I gain some new light, which, at my period of life, I do not expect.

" I am yours truly,

" DANIEL SHARP."

Rev. R. Furman, D. D., South Carolina, to the governor of the state, 1833 :—

" The right of holding slaves is clearly established in the Holy Scriptures, both by precept and example."

On the death of Dr. F., which occurred soon after, among the property advertised by his executor to be sold at public auction, was a " library of miscellaneous character, chiefly theological, twenty-seven NEGROES, some of them very prime, two mules, one horse, and an old wagon." Query—Were any of the Negroes, whom Dr. Furman left at his death, to be sold at auction with his mules and horse, his own children? I am much inclined to think they were. For the doctor derives his sanction for holding slaves from the "example" of the patriarchs; and if my memory serves me, they made concubines of their handmaids. I know of no good reason why their example should not serve in the one case, as well as in the other. Nor will the revelations which have been made within the past few years warrant me in thinking that our modern doctors of divinity would be less likely to imitate the example of Abraham, in the *use* which he made of his *property*, Hagar, than in his *claim* to her, as such. I know nothing of the private habits of Dr. Furman, but he was a *slaveholder* and an *advocate of slavery ;* and I have already shown that every slaveholder is an *adulterer;* nay, that he is guilty of a crime of a much deeper dye. I should be afraid to trust a friend of mine in the company of any man who would sell, or hold, her, or any other woman, as a slave! Such a man is a libertine at heart, and has not the least possible regard for female chastity; otherwise he could never consent to see, much less to hold, any of the sex in the helpless and unprotected condition of a slave. It is proper to add that Dr. Furman was president of the Baptist General Convention a short time previous to his death.

The Charleston Baptist Association (extract of an Address to the Legislature of South Carolina) :

"The question, it is believed, is purely one of political economy. It amounts, in effect, to this— *Whether the operatives of a country shall be bought and sold, and themselves become property, as in this state; or whether they shall be hirelings, and their labor only become property, as in some other states ;* in other words, whether an employer may buy the whole time of lab rers at once, of those who have a right to dispose of it, with a permanent relation of protection and care over them, or whether he shall be restricted to buy it in certain portions only, subject to their control, and with no such permanent relation of care and protection. *The right of masters to dispose of the time of their slaves has been distinctly recognized by the Creator of all things,* who is surely at liberty to vest the right of property over any object in whomsover he pleases. That the lawful possessor should retain this right at will, is no more against the laws of society and good morals, than that he should retain the personal endowments with which his Creator has blessed him, or the money and lands inherited from his ancestors, or acquired by his industry."

What will the working men and women of the North say to this doctrine of the Baptist clergy that "the operatives of a country shall be bought and sold, and themselves become *prop-*

*erty*"? At the South, many of the Baptist brethren are the property of their priests: are the Northern brethren ready to become the property of theirs? Dr. Bolles and Dr. Sharp, who are now enjoying "a pleasing degree of union" with this same Charleston Baptist Association, would doubtless be glad to *own* some of them. They are now nothing but " HIRELINGS," in the estimation of the Charleston Association: would it not suit as well, if a slight change were made in their relations, so that, instead of being "*hirelings*," as at present, they should become the *property* of their employers? I am amazed that any working man or woman in the country can look upon the Baptist church with any other feelings than those of abhorrence and alarm! These ministers would sell every soul of them into slavery, if they had the power to do it; for they have no more regard for *their* rights and liberty, than they have for those they *now* hold in bondage.

The Goslien Association, Virginia:—

Resolved,—

" 1. That we consider our right and title to this property [slaves] altogether legal and *bona fide*, and that it is a breach of the faith pledged in the Federal Constitution, for our Northern brethren to try, either directly or indirectly, to lessen the value of this property, or impair our title thereto."

Resolved,—

" 2. That we view [in the movements of the abolitionists] the torch of the incendiary, and the dagger of the midnight assassin, loosely concealed under the specious garb of humanity and religion, falsely so called."

The Savannah River Baptist Association, in reply to the question,—

" Whether, in the case of involuntary separation, of such a character as to preclude all prospect of future intercourse, the parties ought to be allowed to marry again."

*Answer,* —

" That such separation among persons situated as our slaves are, is *civilly* a separation by *death*, and they believe that, in the sight of God, it would be so viewed. To forbid second marriages in such cases, would be to expose the parties, not only to stronger hardships and strong temptation, but to *church censure*, for acting in obedience to their masters, who cannot be expected to acquiesce in a regulation at variance with justice to the slaves, and to the spirit of that command which regulates marriage among Christians. *The slaves are not free agents*, and a dissolution by death is not more entirely without their consent, and beyond their control, by such separation."

Hung be the heavens in sackcloth!—Let the sun hide his face in darkness, as when the infatuated Jews nailed the Son of God to the cross!—and let there be a jubilee in Hell!—What have we here? An ecclesiastical decision which sets the authority of Jehovah at nought, and blots out the heaven-ordained institution of marriage among 2,700,000 of our own countrymen!—the decree of a council of Baptist clergymen in favor of second marriages, whilst both the parties to the original are still living!! These vile hypocrites are not satisfied with tearing asunder the loving pair whom God has joined in holy wedlock, and forcing them to take to their bosoms other companions whom they cannot love, and *should* not, if they could; but they must make God accessory to the infernal deed. They gravely tell us, that he regards it as "a separation by *death*," and, of course, that he will hold them guiltless. This is the religion of the Baptist church! These are the men with whom Dr. Bolles assures us the multiplying thousands of Baptists throughout the country are enjoying *a pleasing degree of union.*

If there be a God in heaven who takes cognizance of the actions of men, and if there be in reserve a place of punishment for the guilty, where every one shall receive his due reward, I think the day of final retribution must be a *trying* one to the Baptist church. No crime was ever perpetrated by depraved mortals which, as a body, they have not sanctioned. They have wrested the sceptre of dominion from the hand of Jehovah, abrogated his law, and made themselves the supreme sovereigns of thousands of his children, whose bodies and souls they have converted into merchandise, and now offer for sale in market with the neighing horse and lowing ox.

They have annihilated the sacred institution of marriage, and legalized adultery and rape in their most odious and hateful forms, making thousands of the female members of their own church the Breeders on their plantations, whose offspring are torn from them with as little reluctance as the calf is torn from the cow!—Their crimes would put Atheism itself to the blush. Did ever Thomas Paine or Abner Kneeland advocate forced concubinage? Did they ever contend for man's right to unlimited power over woman? But this is advocated by the Baptist church. Slavery is nothing but a system of forced concubinage and adultery! It gives woman up into the power of her owner, to do with her as he pleases! Thousands of the Baptists of this country claim, and *exercise*, this power over the female sex; and more than nine tenths of the remainder authorize their claim and assist them to maintain it.

Can any woman in the Baptist church be pure in heart? I
3*

think not, if she possess sufficient intelligence to understand the nature of her church relations. She is an adulteress *at heart;* otherwise she could not fellowship a church which had annihilated the marriage institution, and thrown a million of her sisters into the market for purposes of prostitution. By her fellowship of slaveholders, she shows that she has, at heart, no abhorrence of an adulterous connection; and if she is herself kept from it, it is only by the force of external circumstances. If Jeremiah could say of the Jewish church in his day, that they were "*all adulterers*," with how much more force and propriety may this charge be brought against the Baptist church, whose most distinguished ministers "have given a boy for a harlot, and sold a girl for wine, that they might drink!" nay to have even *sold* GIRLS *for wine for their communion table!!*—But I must leave this painful picture, and turn to

## THE PROTESTANT EPISCOPAL CHURCH.

Of this church I have little to say; for, from the very nature of its organization, and the character of the elements of which it is composed, it is the very last of all the sects to which any cause of reform should look for aid. From the commencement of our enterprise, it has been an inveterate enemy of abolition, and has thrown its entire influence, as a body, into the scale of slavery. Among its members have been found a few sterling abolitionists, but fewer probably, in proportion to its whole numbers, than in any other denomination. I believe the first instance of the opening its meeting-houses for anti-slavery lectures is yet to be recorded; and if, in its ecclesiastical capacity, it has done less to sustain slavery, by positive action in its favor, than some of the other sects, it has not been for want of love for the system, but from its haughty and dignified indifference to all matters of general interest. Many of its ministers and members are slave-claimants, and nearly all of them legalize slavery, and strenuously oppose its abolition in the District of Columbia; and in abusive treatment of people of color, they have, if possible, rivalled even the Methodist church.

Some idea of the spirit which pervades this body towards that portion of our countrymen to whom God has given a complexion differing from ours, may be gathered from the following extracts from a recent work from the pen of Judge Jay, himself a Churchman, entitled "Caste and Slavery in the American Church."

Mr. Jay says:—

"In the month of June, 1839, the Board of Trustees of the General Theological Seminary, composed of the bishops and clerical and lay delegates from the different states and territories, met at New York; and their proceedings were subsequently published in a pamphlet. From the minutes, it appears that a candidate for holy orders in the diocese of New York, now the Rev. ALEXANDER CRUMMELL, applied to them, by petition, to be allowed to enter the seminary as a student; that the petition was referred to a committee consisting of the Right Rev. Bp. H. U. ONDERDONK, Rev. Drs. JAMES MILNOR and HUGH SMITH, and WM. JOHNSON, DAVID B. OGDEN, and EDWARD A. NEWTON, Esquires, who, after deliberate consideration, recommended a resolution of rejection, which, on the motion of the Rev. FRANCIS L. HAWKES, D. D., was adopted; that the Right Rev. Bishop DOANE asked leave to enter his protest against the decision, and that leave was not granted. Neither the reasons for their decision, nor the disqualification of the candidate, are even intimated by the minutes; but it does appear, that the right of every candidate for orders to enter the seminary was expressly guaranteed by the constitution, which the trustees were bound to obey; and that this fact was well known to them, also appears from an amendment proposed by the bishop of New York, while the matter was pending, to the very clause upon which they were trampling.

"The true cause which led the trustees to nullify the constitution and deny the right of the candidate, and which they were ashamed to acknowledge, was, that he was a *colored* man; and this was the *only* cause—his diocesan, Bishop Onderdonk, of New York, having declared in 'The Churchman' (Nov. 4. 1839), that he explicitly stated to them, 'that if they should think it right and proper to admit a COLORED MAN into the Seminary, he considered the applicant before them *one in whose case it might with great safety and propriety be done.*'

"The Rev. Peter Williams, for many years a respectable clergyman of New York, was never allowed to sit as a member of the Diocesan Convention, nor has the Church of St. Philip, of which he was the pastor, been yet represented in that body. He died soon after the act of the trustees, upon which we have been remarking, was exposed to the world; and to counteract, as far as possible, the indignation it had excited, the clergy in a body, attended his funeral, and the bishop of New York pronounced from the pulpit a high eulogium upon his character. Several of the clergy admitted that it was done merely for effect, and one of them bitterly remarked at the funeral, that the empty honors to the lifeless dust were a poor atonement for the insults so often offered to the living man. The Rev. Mr. DeGrasse, another colored clergyman of the Episcopal church, of fine talents, excellent acquirements, and amiable disposition,—who, three years previously to the application of Mr. Crummell, had been excluded from the Seminary, and who, after a residence of some years in this city, sought in the West Indies the respectful treatment and sympathy he could not find at home, and there ended his early years by a Christian's death,—once said to the writer, with tears in his eyes, 'I feel that the bishop and many of the clergy are against us—that they do not want any colored clergymen in the church. I have struggled against the conviction, but it is impossible to resist it; the proofs are too strong; I experience it daily; I know it is so.'

"In the diocese of Pennsylvania, an express canon debars the African church from being represented in the Convention, and excludes the rector from a seat. Truly! a singular picture to be exhibited by Christians meeting as a council of the church; but the limits of caste stop not here. Beautifully says the poet—

'Are we not brothers?
So man and man should be;
But clay and clay differs in dignity,
*Whose dust is both alike.*'

"Since Shakspeare wrote, even the *dust* has learned to claim precedence over dust; and *Noli me tangere* is daintily inscribed upon the mouldering coffin-lid.

"Ay! this 'aristocracy of color' is maintained not only in God's temples, but even in that last abode where all distinctions have been supposed to disappear. In the very graveyard where Death reigns as conqueror, and worms revel on the mouldering remains of manliness and beauty; where pride, and pomp, and power, have doffed their trappings, and have said to corruption, Thou art my father, and to the worms, Thou art my mother and my sister; where the voice of passion is forever stilled, and the heart that has ceased to beat is as cold as the marble beneath which it reposes;—even here, among the tombs, Prejudice has his dwelling, like the demoniac of old, and Caste, under the sanction of the church, rears its hideous and revolting form. How many similar instances there may be, we know not; that we cite has come under our immediate notice. The vestry and wardens of an Episcopal church in the diocese of New York, a few years since, accepted a deed for a cemetery, which was demised to them upon the express condition embodied in the indenture, '*that they should never suffer any colored person to be buried in any part of the same;*' and all the subsequent conveyances on the part of the church, of vaults and burial-places, are subject to the same conditions."

## THE UNITARIAN AND UNIVERSALIST CHURCHES.

Whoever has bestowed an hour's serious reflection on the nature and tendency of ecclesiastical institutions, will see that these churches have much less power to harm any work of reform, than those sects which are called evangelical. From the looseness of their organization, and the Anti-Pharisaic character of their professions, their ecclesiastical influence is comparatively limited, either for good or for evil. Their influence is more that of the individual; and in relation to slavery, they stand much nearer the position of non-church commrnicants, than do the other sects. But still they have an ecclesiastical existence and, of course, some ecclesiastical influence; and that influence, however trifling it may have been, has all been given in support of slavery. As a body, they have given the anti-slavery cause no countenance. The least that can in truth be said of them is, that, ecclesiastically, they have walked in the footsteps of the priest and the Levite, straight by the poor, bleeding slave, on the other side, or have turned aside only to cast a cold and heartless look upon his wretchedness; while in the capacity of citizens, they have joined his oppressors, and assisted in stripping him of his rights, and plundering his domestic hearthstone. And as they profess to be Christians, and members of the church of Christ, and at the same time *legalize slavery and the slave trade*, and also fellowship slave-claimants as Christians, there is no *essential* difference between them and the other sects. They are all under the same condemnation, and are alike the enemies of truth and impartial freedom.

## THE FREE-WILL BAPTISTS AND THE SOCIETY OF FRIENDS.

These sects, like all the others, when weighed in the balance of truth, are found wanting. As bodies, they claim to be anti-slavery; but their claim is like that of the Pharisee, who thanked God that he was not like that publican who stood by his side, when at the same time he was the more guilty of the two. It is true that they have *spoken* against slavery; and spoken, too, in strong terms of reprobation; but it is equally true, that with both hands they have upheld it; and they now stand before the world in a more reprehensible light than any of the other sects. From motives of self interest, or an unwillingness to depart from a rule introduced by their fathers, they admit no slave-claimant to their fellowship; but at the same time, as a body, they stand entirely aloof from the anti-slavery enterprise, or openly oppose it. And while sending forth to the world their resolutions and testimonies against slavery, they *legalize* it, and do whatever lies in their power to render it popular, and consequently permanent, by electing man-stealers to fill the highest offices in the government. At the ballot-box, no sect in the land is more notoriously subservient to the slave power than the Free-Will Baptists.

In New Hampshire, where they are very numerous, they are principally connected with the Democratic party; and it was chiefly through their instrumentality, that that poor *apology* for a man, Charles G. Atherton, was returned to Congress, after having disgraced himself and his country by consenting to be made a cat's-paw by Southern *slave-breeders*, to tear in pieces the sacred right of petition! It was in their power to prevent his reëlection. and return to Congress a thorough-going abolitionist in his stead; but *he* was the man of their choice! And yet, at this very time, they were passing flaming resolutions against slavery. and making loud professions of abolitionism!

I have said that the American church and clergy, as a body, were PIRATES. Is this charge true, so far as it relates to the Free-Will Baptists and Quakers? It is, if *aiding* and *abetting* pirates, and protecting them while engaged in perpetrating their atrocities, constitutes one a pirate; for both of these sects legalize and protect a species of commerce in the United States, which they have declared to be piracy, when carried on upon the coast of Africa. Am I told that they have acted *ignorantly* in this matter? My reply is, if they are men of common-sense, they must and do know that voting for slave-claimants and the advocates and supporters of slavery to legislate for the country, tends to perpetuate the bloody system. Would they vote for such men if their own wives and children were in slavery? So long as they are connected with slaveholding political parties, their resolutions and testimonies against slavery only serve to enhance their guilt, and aggravate their condemnation.

If the government had instituted a system of idol worship, and a hundred oxen were daily offered in sacrifice on the altar of some distinguished god, in the city of Washington, by an order of Congress, what would you say of that religious sect, who should pass *resolves* against idolatry, and at the same time vote for men to represent them in Congress who were opposed to the abolition of these sacrifices, and also elect a high-priest of this deity to fill the presidential chair? But such conduct would not be more hypocritical and reprehensible than the conduct of the Free-Will Baptists and Friends, and the other religious bodies that have adopted resolutions against slavery!

The remarks which I have made upon the Free-Will Baptists and Friends, will apply with equal force to those branches of other sects which have adopted resolutions against slavery. This kind of action, so long as they stand connected with pro-slavery parties, either political or ecclesiastical, only renders their influence more formidable to the anti-slavery enterprise; and consequently their guilt is proportionably increased. They tell us that slavery is a heinous sin and crime, and yet act in concert with those who advocate and uphold it! Hence, on their own confession, they are the "*companions of thieves*," and in fellowship with adulterers. In my general charges, therefore, against the sects, no exception is required in favor of those local churches which claim to be anti-slavery, on the ground of having adopted anti-slavery resolutions, while they are still connected with their respective sectarian denominations, and in Christian fellowship with those who act in concert with pro-slavery political parties. The least that can in truth be said of such churches is, that they are the LUKEWARM friends of the slave, whom God will *spew out of his mouth.*

I had intended to speak, in this connection, of the character and tendency of our so-called benevolent institutions; but having already far exceeded the limits which I originally proposed to myself in this letter, I must pass them by with the single remark, that connected with the Boards of most of them are more or less slave-claimants, and their treasuries are polluted with the price of human blood!—and that the money which our clergy beg of poor widows to send the gospel to the heathen, goes into the hands of such men as Rev. Wm. S. Plummer, D. D., the man who called upon the Richmond mob to "catch" the abolitionists and give them a "WARMING AT THE FIRE!" For the same reason, I have also omitted to notice several of the smaller religious denominations. I would here say of them, however, that they are all composed of sectarians, and not abolitionists; and hence they belong to the same category with the larger and more influential sects, and should be regarded in a similar light.

But I trust I have already adduced abundant evidence on this heart-rending subject, to substantiate my allegations against the American church and clergy. With this picture before him, no one, I think, will say that I have done them injustice. True, I have brought against them the most tremendous charges! I have denounced them, as a body, as THIEVES, ADULTERERS, MAN-STEALERS, PIRATES, and MURDERERS! But who, in view of the frightful and accumulated proof of their guilt, which I have here presented, can deny these charges? Who, that has a mind capable of understanding the political and ecclesiastical connection

of the church and clergy with the slave system, as I have here
portrayed it, and can comprehend the direful consequences of
that connection, will dare to say that God will hold them guiltless of these crimes ?   Gladly would I believe them innocent;
but reason, conscience, and my outraged sense of justice, all
forbid the thought.

I will close this part of my argument with a few specimens of
the fruits of slavery, as it exists in the midst, and under the control, of the religious influences of the country.   As your eye
glances over the horrible picture which I am about to present,
bear in mind that it is the legitimate and inevitable result of the
system which the church and clergy generally not only legalize,
but baptize into the name of the Father, and of the Son, and of
the Holy Ghost.   It is heart-rending, indeed, to see humanity
thus mangled and bruised ; but so it must ever be until slavery
itself shall be abolished ; for it cannot exist without the exercise
of the most horrible cruelties.   It is only in the presence of
whips, and chains, and branding-irons, that the slave will submit
to his degraded condition.

The following advertisements are from Southern newspapers,
and are only a very few of the many thousands of similar ones,
which blacken the columns of the Southern press :

"Committed to jail as a runaway, a negro woman named
Martha, 17 or 18 years of age—has *numerous scars of the whip* on
her back."        D. JUDD, Jailor, Davidson County, Tenn.

"Ten dollars reward for my woman Siby, *very much scarred
about the neck and ears by whipping.*"
                                    ROBERT NICHOLL, Mobile, Ala.

"Ran away, a negro woman, named Maria—*some scars on her
back, occasioned by the whip.*"
              BRYANT JOHNSON, Fort Valley, Houston County, Ga.

"Stolen, a negro woman, named Celia—on examining her
back, you will find *marks caused by the whip.*"
            JAMES T. DEJARNETT, Vernon, Autauga County, Tenn.

"Lodged in jail, a mulatto boy, *having large marks of the whip*
on his shoulders and other parts of his body."
                                    MAURICE V GARCIA,
                          Sheriff of the County of Jefferson, La.

"Was committed, a negro boy named Tom—*is much marked
with the whip.*"
              R. J. BLAND, Sheriff of Claiborne County, Miss.

"Ran away a negro fellow named Dick—has *many scars* on his back from being *whipped*."

JAMES NOE, Red River Landing, La.

"Committed to jail, a negro slave; his back is *very badly scarred*."  WILLIAM CRAZE, Jailor, Alexandria, La.

"Committed a mulatto fellow—his back *shows lasting impressions of the whip*, and leaves no doubt of his being a SLAVE."

JOHN A. ROWLAND, Jailor, Lumberton, N. C.

"Committed to jail, a negro man—his back *much marked* by the whip."  J. K. ROBERTS, Sheriff, Blount County, Ala.

"Ran away, the negro slave named Jupiter—has a *fresh mark* of a cowskin on one of his cheeks."  H. VARILLAT, N. O.

"Ran away, a negro man named Johnson—he has *a great many marks of the whip* on his back."

CORNELIUS D. TOLIN, Augusta, Ga.

"Ran away, Bill—has *several* LARGE SCARS on his back, from a *severe* whipping in *early* life."

JOHN WATTON, Rockville, Montgomery County, Md.

"Ran away, a boy named Jim—with the marks of the *whip* on the small of the back, reaching round to the flank."

SAMUEL STEWART, Greensboro', Ala.

"Brought to Jail, a negro man named George—he has a *great many scars from the lash*."

S. B. MURPHY, Sheriff, Wilkinson County, Ga.

"Was committed to jail, a yellow boy named Jim—had on a *large lock chain around his neck*."

WILLIAM TOLER, Sheriff of Simpson County, Miss.

"Ran away, a negro named David—with some *iron hobbles around each ankle*."  HASLET LOFLANO, Staunton, Va.

"Ran away, negress Caroline—had on a *collar with one prong turned down*."  T. ENGGY, New Orleans.

"Ran away, a black woman, Betsey—had an *iron bar on her right leg*."  JOHN HENDERSON, Washington County, Mi.

"Was committed to jail, a negro named Ambrose—has a *ring of iron around his neck*."

WILLIAM DYER, Sheriff, Claiborne, La.

"Ran away, a negro man named Charles—had on a *drawing chain*, fastened around his ankle with a house lock."

FRANCIS DURETT, Lexington, Lauderdale County, Ala.

" Ran away, the negro Manual, *much marked with irons.*"

A. MURAT, Baton Rouge.

" Was committed to jail, a negro boy—had on a *large neck iron,* with a *huge pair of horns, and a large bar or band of iron* on his left leg."

H. GRIDLEY, Sheriff of Adams County, Mi.

" Ran away, the negro George—he had on *his neck an iron collar,* the branches of which had been taken off."

FERDINAND LEMOS, New Orleans.

" Committed to jail, a man who calls his name John—he has *a clog of iron on his right foot which will weigh four or five pounds* " B. W. HODGES, Jailor, Pike County, Ala.

" Detained at the police Jail, the negro wench Myra—has several marks of *lashing,* and has *irons on her feet.*"

P. BAYHI, Captain of the Police.

Ran away, Betsey—when she left she had on her *neck an iron collar.*" CHARLES KERNAN, Parish of Jefferson, La.

" Ran away, a negro woman and two children—a few days before she went off *I burnt her with a hot iron,* on the left side of her face : I *tried to make the letter M.*"

MICAJAH RICH, Nash County, N. C.

" Ran away, Mary, a black woman—has a *scar* on her back and right arm near the shoulder, *caused by a rifle ball.*"

ASA B. MELCALF, Kingston, Adams County, Mi.

" Ran away, a negro man named Henry, *his left eye out,* some scars from *dirk* on and under his left arm, and *much scarred* with the whip."

WILLIAM OVERSTREET, Benton, Yazoo Co., Mi.

" Ran away, Sam—he was *shot* a short time since through the hand, and has *several shots in his left arm and side.*"

O. W. LAINS, Ark.

" Ran away, my negro man Dennis—said negro has been *shot* in his left arm, between the shoulder and elbow, which has paralyzed the left hand." R. W. SIZER, Mi.

" Ran away, my negro man named Simon—he *has been shot badly* in his back and right arm."

NICHOLAS EDMUNDS, Va.

" Ran away, a negro girl called Mary—has a small scar over her eye, a *good many teeth missing*—the letter A *is branded on her cheek and forehead.*"

J. P. ASHFORD, Adams County, Mi.

"Committed, a negro man—is *very badly shot in the right side* and right hand." S. B. MURPHY, Jailor, Irvington, Ga.

" Ran away, a negro man named Ned—*three of his fingers* are drawn into the palm of his hand by a *cut*—has a *scar* on the back of his neck nearly half round, done by a *knife.*"

ISAAC JOHNSON, Pulaski county, Ga.

" Was committed to jail, a negro man—says his name is Josiah,; his back is very much scarred by whip, and *branded on the thigh and hips, in three or four places*, thus, J. M.,—the *rim of his right ear has been bit or cut off.*"

J. L. JOLLEY, Sheriff of Clinton County, Mi.

" Fifty dollars' reward for my fellow Edward—he has a *scar* on the corner of his mouth, two *cuts* on and under his arm, and the *letter* E *on his arm.*"

THOMAS LEDWITH, Jacksonville, East Florida.

" Ran away, Anthony—one of his *ears cut off*, and his left hand cut with an ax." STEPHEN M. JACKSON.

" Ran away, Gabriel—has *two or three scars across his neck*, made with a knife."

LEMUEL MILES, Steen's Creek, Rankin County, Mi.

" Ran away, my man Fountain—has *holes in his ears*, a *scar* on the right side of his forehead—has been *shot in the hind parts of his legs*—is marked in the back with the whip."

ROBERT BEASLEY, Macon, Ga.

"TWENTY DOLLARS' REWARD. Ran away from the subscriber, on the 14th instant, a negro girl named Molly. She is 16 or 17 years of age, slim made, LATELY BRANDED ON THE LEFT CHEEK, THUS R, AND A PIECE TAKEN OFF OF HER EAR ON THE SAME SIDE ; THE SAME LETTER BRANDED ON THE INSIDE OF BOTH HER LEGS." ABNER ROSS, Fairfield District, S. C.

The Wilmington (North Carolina) *Advertiser*, of July 13, 1838, contains the following advertisement :—

" RAN AWAY, my negro man RICHARD. A reward of $25 will be paid for his apprehension, DEAD or ALIVE. Satisfactory proof will only be required of his being KILLED. He has with him, in all probability, his wife ELIZA, who ran away from Col. Thompson, now a resident of Alabama, about the time he commenced his journey to that state." D. H. RHODES.

In the Macon (Georgia) *Telegraph*, May 28, is the following :—

"About the 1st of March last, the negro man RANSOM left me without the least provocation whatever. I will give a reward of

$20 for said negro, if taken DEAD or ALIVE,—and if killed in any attempt, an advance of $5 will be paid.

"Crawford Co., Ga.                                        BRYANT JOHNSON."

On the 28th of April, 1836, a colored man, named McIntosh, was seized by a mob, in the city of St. Louis, fastened to a tree in the midst of the city, in open day, and burnt to death, in the presence of an immense throng of citizens, who had assembled to give their countenance to the deed. The Alton (Ill.) *Telegraph* contains the following notice of the scene:—

"All was silent as death while the executioners were piling wood around their victim. He said not a word, until feeling that the flames had seized upon him. Then he uttered an awful howl, attempting to sing and pray, then hung his head, and suffered in silence, except in the following instance: After the flames had surrounded their prey, his eyes burnt out of his head, and his mouth seemingly parched to a cinder, some one in the crowd, more compassionate than the rest, proposed to put an end to his misery by shooting him, when it was replied, ' That would be of no use, since he was already out of pain.' ' No, no,' said the wretch, ' I am not. I am suffering as much as ever ; shoot me, shoot me.' ' No, no,' said one of the fiends, who was standing about the sacrifice they were roasting, ' he shall not be shot. *I would sooner slacken the fire, if that would increase his misery ;* and the man who said this, was, as we understand, AN OFFICER OF JUSTICE."

The following scene is related by Rev. James A. Thome, son of Arthur Thome, of Augusta, Ky. :—

"In December of 1833, I landed at New Orleans, in the steamer W———. It was after night, dark and rainy. The passengers were called out of the cabin, from the enjoyment of a fire, which the cold, damp atmosphere rendered very comfortable, by a sudden shout of 'Catch him—catch him—catch the negro.' The cry was answered by a hundred voices—' Catch him—*kill* him ;' and a rush from every direction toward our boat indicated that the object of pursuit was near. The next moment we heard a man plunge into the river a few paces above us. A crowd gathered upon the shore, with lamps, and stones, and clubs, still crying, ' Catch him—kill him—catch him—shoot him.'

" I soon discovered the poor man. He had taken refuge under the prow of another boat, and was standing in the water up to his waist. The angry vociferation of his pursuers did not intimidate him. He defied them all. ' Don't you *dare* to come near me, or I will sink you in the river.' He was armed with despair. For a moment the mob were palsied by the energy of his threatenings. They were afraid to go to him with a skiff, but a num-

ber of them went on to the boat, and tried to seize him. They
threw a noose-rope down repeatedly *that they might pull him up
by the neck!* but he planted his hand firmly against the boat, and
dashed the rope away with his arms. One of them took a long
bar of wood, and, leaning over the prow, endeavored to strike
him on the head. The blow must have shattered the skull, but
it did not reach low enough. The monster raised up the heavy
club again, and said, ' Come out now, you old rascal, or die.'
' Strike,' said the negro; ' strike—shiver my brains *now;* I want
to die;' and down went the club again, without striking. This
was repeated several times. The mob, seeing their efforts fruit-
less, became more enraged, and threatened to stone him, if he did
not surrender himself into their hands. He again defied them,
and declared he would drown himself in the river, before they
should have him. They then resorted to persuasion, and promised
they would not hurt him. ' I'll die first,' was his only reply.
Even the furious mob was awed, and for a while stood dumb.

"After standing in the cold water for an hour, the miserable
being began to fail. We observed him gradually sinking—his
voice grew weak and tremulous—yet he continued to *curse!* In
the midst of his oaths he uttered broken sentences,—' I didn't
steal the meat—I didn't steal—my master lives—master—master
lives up the river—[his voice began to gurgle in his throat, and
he was so chilled that his teeth chattered audibly]—I didn't—
steal—I didn't steal—my—my master—my—-I want to see my
master—I didn't—no—my mas—you want—you want to kill
me—I didn't steal the—' His last words could just be heard as
he sank under the water."

The Natchez *Free Trader*, of June, 1842, gives the following
account of the burning of a negro at Union Point, Miss. :—

"The body was taken and chained to a tree immediately on the
bank of the Mississippi, on what is called Union Point. Fagots
were then collected, and piled around him, to which he appeared
quite indifferent. When the work was completed, he was asked
what he had to say. He then warned all to take example by him,
and asked the prayers of all around ; he then called for a drink
of water, which was handed to him ; he drank it, and said, 'Now
set fire—I am ready to go in peace !' The torches were lighted and
placed in the pile, which soon ignited He watched unmoved
the curling flame, that grew until it began to entwine itself
around and feed upon his body ; then he sent forth cries of agony
painful to the ear, begging some one to blow his brains out; at
the same time surging with almost superhuman strength, until
the staple with which the chain was fastened to the tree (not being well secured) drew out, and he leaped from the burning pile.
At that moment the sharp ringing of several rifles was heard ; the

body of the negro fell a corpse to the ground. He was picked up by some two or three, and again thrown into the fire and consumed—not a vestige remaining to show that such a being ever existed.

STATE OF NORTH CAROLINA, }
Lenoir County. }

" Whereas, complaint hath been this day made to us, two of the justices of peace for the said county, by William D. Cobb, of Jones county, that two negro slaves belonging to him, named BEN (oommonly known by the name of *Ben Fox*) and RIG-DON, have absented themselves from their said master's service, and are lurking about in the counties of Lenoir and Jones, committing acts of felony ;—these are, in the name of the state, to command the said slaves forthwith to surrender themselves, and return home to their said master. And we do also hereby require the sheriff of said county of Lenoir to make diligent search and pursuit after the above-mentioned slaves; and them having found, to apprehend and secure so that they may be conveyed to their said master, or otherwise discharged as the law directs. And the said sheriff is hereby empowered to raise and take with him such power of his county as he shall think fit for the apprehension of said slaves. And we do hereby, by virtue of an act of the Assembly of this state, concerning servants and slaves, intimate and declare, if the said slaves do not surrender themselves, and return home to their master immediately after the publication of these presents, *that any person may kill and destroy said slaves by such means as he or they think fit. without accusation or impeachment of any crime or offence for so doing, or without incurring any penalty or forfeiture thereby.*

" Given under our hands and seals, this 12th of November, 1836. 　　　　　　　　　　　　B. COLEMAN, J. P. [Seal].
　　　　　　　　　　　　　　　JAS JONES, J. P." [Seal.]

200 DOLLARS' REWARD —Ran away from the subscriber, about three years ago, a certain negro man named Ben (commonly known by the name of Ben Fox). Also one other negro, by the name of Rigdon, who ran away on the 8th of this month.

I will give the reward of one hundred dollars for each of the above negroes, to be delivered to me or confined in the jail of Lenoir or Jones county, or *for the killing of them so that I can see them.* 　　　　　　　　　　　　　　　　　　W. D. COBB.
November 12, 1836.

I will only add in this connection, that these atrocious outrages were mostly perpetrated under the sanctions of American law ; and in no solitary instance have the perpetrators been brought to condign punishment. Indeed, they are but the legitimate offspring of the slave system, and are inseparable from it. And yet

Prof. Stuart tells us that that system "may exist, and that, too, without violating the Christian faith;" and the *Hon.* Edward Everett (a church mumber), once, on the floor of Congress, volunteered *military* aid in its defence. " Sir," said he, addressing the speaker, "I am no soldier. My habits and education are very unmilitary. But there is no cause in which I would sooner buckle a knapsack on my back, and put a musket on my shoulder, than that of putting down a servile insurrection at the South, * * * Domestic slavery is not, in my judgment, to be set down as an immoral or irreligious relation."

I have now done with the proof which I intend to present in support of my first charge, and come to the second, which is, "That the Methodist Episcopal church is more corrupt than any house of ill-fame in he city of New York." To convince you of the truth of this charge will require no labored argument. The case needs but to be stated, to be fully proved. Those dens of infamy in New York, where the libertine resorts to satiate his depraved desires, are tenanted by women who devote themselves to purposes of prostitution. But are these abandoned characters *compelled* to lives of infamy and crime? Is there for them no escape from the paths of vice? Can they not, on the other hand, change their course, and lead a virtuous life, whenever they choose to do so? But in the Methodist church there are 50,000 women who are inevitably doomed to lives of prostitution. With *them* there is no alternative. They are sold in the market for the domestic SERAGLIO,—they are the " BREEDERS " on the plantation, and are compelled, on pain of cruel scourging, and even death, to submit to their owners' wishes, whatever they may be! And yet this church has assured us, through its highest ecclesiastical tribunal, by a vote of 120 to 14, that it has " *no* WISH *or* INTENTION *to interfere in their civil and political relations!* " It *would* not place them in a situation where their virtue would be secure against the brutal marauder, if it could! The church, as a body, sanctions, and great numbers of its members perpetrate on their slaves, the very crime which the laws of your state punish with *death!*

My third charge is, " That the Southern ministers of the Methodist Episcopal church are desirous of perpetuating slavery, for the purpose of supplying themselves with concubines from among its hapless victims." From the nature of the case, the proof of this allegation must necessarily be circumstantial. But it is not, on that account, the less satisfactory; for men never act but from motives; and the actions are a sure index to the state of the heart. The tree is known by its fruit. In charging the Southern ministry with a desire to perpetuate slavery for the purpose of supplying themselves with concubines, I do not assert that this is their *only* motive in supporting it, but that it is *a* motive!

Now, that these men are desirous of perpetuating slavery, there can be no manner of doubt; for they tell us plainly that they have no *wish* to see it abolished. They must, therefore, have some motive in wishing to perpetuate it. That motive, surely, cannot be a sincere desire to spread the knowledge of Jesus Christ, and the triumphs of his kingdom; nor can it be love of wealth,—that master passion of the human breast,—for slavery is fast bankrupting the whole South. Nor is it found in their love of reputation, nor yet in their regard for the quietude of domestic life; for these would both be greatly enhanced by the abolition of slavery. It is, doubtless, found in part, however, in their love of power; but is this their only inducement? Is it from a desire of domination alone that they sustain a system which their founder denounced as the "sum of all villanies," and which is fast filling the land with pauperism, ignorance, and crime? That surely cannot be. There is a stronger motive in this matter than the love of power; and that motive is revealed to us in the history of the private morals of our Northern clergy. If Northern ministers possess such strong predilections for adultery and concubinage, as the painful disclosures of the few past years force us to believe, hedged about as they are, on every side with the safeguards of virtue; if they are often willing to hazard the loss of reputation, and even the disgrace and sufferings of incarceration in the state penitentiary, to gratify those predilections,—is it not natural to suppose, nay, is it not morally certain, that the Southern clergy, nursed as they have been in the very hotbeds of pollution, would be anxious to perpetuate a system which affords them ample scope for indulgence, without danger, or even the fear of disgrace? That such is the fact, is abundantly proved by the adoption, by the General Conference of 1840, of the resolution denying to persons of color "the right to testify against white persons, in cases of church discipline." Pending a motion to reconsider that infamous resolution, the strongest remonstrances were urged against it by Southern ministers, who even went so far as to threaten a dissolution of the church, if the resolution should be rescinded. I must give you a specimen of their expostulations. They betray a sensitiveness and warmth of feeling, as you will perceive, which no other question has ever called forth.

The Rev. William Winans, of Mississippi, said,—

"He was never more deeply impressed with the solemnity of his situation—the act of this afternoon will determine the fate of our beloved Zion  *  *  *  *  If you wrest from us that resolution, you stab us to the vitals!  *  *  *  *  Repeal that resolution, and you pass the Rubicon!  Dear as union is, sir, there are interests at stake in this question which are dearer than union!  Do not regard us as threatening  *  *  *  *  But what will become of our beloved Methodism?  The interests of Methodism throughout the whole South are at stake! "

The Rev. Mr. Collins, of ——,

" Admonished the Conference, that the moment they rescinded that resolution, they passed the Rubicon.  The fate of the connection was sealed."

The Rev. William Smith, of Virginia,

" Agreed with the brother from Mississippi, that there were interests involved in this question *dearer* than UNION itself, however dear that might be.  Southerners are not prepared to commit their interests, much less their consciences, to the holy keeping of Northern men.  *Conscience* was involved in this matter, and they could not be coerced "

Whence, I ask, is this mortal fear of *colored* testimony?  Why do the clergy see in it a dagger, that will " stab them to the vitals " ?  What evil have they done, that they would sooner see the " UNION itself " dissolved than permit their sister, whom Christ has washed and cleansed in his own blood, to give utterance to her thoughts, in an assembly of his saints?  What mighty truth lies hidden in the bosom of the slave, that needs but to be revealed to explode the church—" determine the fate of our beloved Zion "—and blast the rising " interests of Methodism throughout the whole South " ?  But one answer can be given to this question, and that answer abundantly confirms the truth of my charge.

I come now to the last charge in the long catalogue of allegations which I have made against the American church and clergy.  It is this—" That many of our clergy are guilty of enormities that would disgrace an Algerine pirate."  And needs this allegation any further proof, after the appalling developments which I have already made?  If so, I challenge a comparison between the conduct of many of the American clergy, and the Algerine pirates.  Look on the darkest page of Moorish history, and tell me, has the Algerine ever sold his sister of the same faith for a " BREEDER " to " STOCK " the plantation of her haughty proprietor with human cattle, perchance the offspring of his own body?  Has he shipped his brother Algerine to a foreign realm, and sold him for a galley-slave, to one of a religion dif-

4

fering from his own? Has he denied to a portion of his own countrymen the right to read the Koran (his Bible), and sold those countrymen into slavery to raise funds to send that same Koran to those who were ignorant of its contents in other lands? Has he ever claimed the wife and daughters of his Mahometan brother as his *property*? Has he robbed the frantic mother of her babe, and with the price of that babe's body and soul replenished his communion cup? Nay, has he even compelled the heart-broken mother, if she observe the ordinances of her religion at all, to drink from that cup the wine which was purchased with her own child's blood? Such enormities even the tongue of calumny dares not impute to the Algerine pirate, in a solitary instance. And yet they are the settled policy of no inconsiderable portion of the American clergy! They stain and darken almost every page of the modern history of the American church; and if generally known, they would render that church a stench in the nostrils of the heathen of every realm on the globe!

My task is done. My pledge is redeemed. I have here drawn a true but painful picture of the American church and clergy. I have proved them to be a BROTHERHOOD OF THIEVES! I have shown that multitudes of them subsist by ROBBERY and make THEFT their trade!—that they plunder the cradle of its precious contents, and rob the youthful lover of his bride!—that they steal "from principle," and teach their people that slavery "is not opposed to the will of God," but "IS A MERCIFUL VISITATION"!—that they excite the mob to deeds of violence, and advocate LYNCH LAW for the suppression of the sacred right of speech!—I have shown that they sell their own sisters in the church for the SERAGLIO, and invest the proceeds of their sales in BIBLES for the heathen!—that they rob the forlorn and despairing mother of her babe, and barter away that babe to the vintner for wine for the Lord's supper! I have shown that nearly all of them *legalize* slavery, with all its barbarous, bitter, burning wrongs, and make PIRACY lawful and honorable commerce; and that they dignify slave-holding, and render it popular, by placing MAN-STEALERS in the Presidential chair! I have shown that those who themselves abstain from these enormities, are in church fellowship with those who perpetrate them; and that, by this connection, they countenance the wrong, and strengthen the hands of the oppressor! I have shown that while with their lips they profess to believe that LIBERTY is God's free and impartial gift to all, and that it is " *inalienable*," they hold 2,500,000 of their own countrymen in the most abject bondage; thus proving to the world, that they are not *Infidels* merely, but blank ATHEISTS—disbelievers in the existence of a God who will hold them accountable for their actions! These allegations are all supported by evidence which none can controvert, and which no impartial mind can doubt. The truth of them is seen on every page of our country's history; and it is deeply *felt* by more than two millions of our enchained countrymen, who now demand their plundered rights at their hands. In making this heart-rending and appalling disclosure of their hypocrisy and crimes, I have spoken with great plainness, and at times with great severity; but it is the severity of truth and love. I have said that *only* which I could not in kindness withhold! and in discharging the painful duty which devolved upon me in this regard, I have had but a single object in view—the redemption of the oppressor from his *guilt*, and the oppressed from his *chains*. To this darling object of my heart, this letter is now dedicated. As it goes out through you, to the public, a voice of terrible warning and admonition to the guilty oppressor, but of conso-lation, as I trust, to the despairing slave, I only ask for it, that it may be received with the same kindness, and read with the same candor, in which it has been written.

With great respect and affection,

Your sincere friend,<br>S. S. FOSTER.

Canterbury, N. H., July, 1843.